Happier Retirement

Grounded in Spirituality

DR ANTONIO LOBO

Copyright © Dr Antonio Lobo 2024

All Scripture quotations are taken from the NRSV Catholic Edition.

Image credits

Front cover photo courtesy of Niki Lobo.
Back cover photo courtesy of Anne Lobo.

Page 6: Monir Uddin Jowel, CC BY-SA 4.0 <https://creativecommons.org/licenses/by-sa/4.0>, via Wikimedia Commons

Page 31: Darko Tepert Donatus, CC BY-SA 2.5 <https://creativecommons.org/licenses/by-sa/2.5>, via Wikimedia Commons

Page 80: RexxS, CC BY-SA 4.0 <https://creativecommons.org/licenses/by-sa/4.0>, via Wikimedia Commons

Published by

Divine Mercy Publications Pty. Ltd.,
P.O. Box 351, Camberwell, Victoria 3124 Australia
Phone: (03) 9830 4386 Email: sales@divinemercy.com.au
Website: www.divinemercy.com.au

Acknowledgments

I gratefully acknowledge the contribution made by Penny Renner, my assistant, in writing this book. Besides her excellent editing skills, she has enabled me to flesh out some of my ideas, especially those relating to spirituality. I also gratefully acknowledge the important role played by my beautiful wife Anne, who has been a motivating force for me in producing this book. And to my cheeky grandson, Rory, who planted the seed in me to write my memoirs for the next generation. I gratefully acknowledge, too, the kind assistance offered to me by John Canavan, whose advice and expertise have made the publication of this book possible. Last, but not the least I gratefully acknowledge the contribution of South Star Design who has meticulously planned the layout and formatting of the entire manuscript.

Finally, the crowning glory has to be awarded to the Holy Spirit, whose continuous guidance and inspiration has made this work possible.

Contents

Endorsements vi

Foreword 1

Introduction 2
    Purpose of writing this book 2
    A synopsis of the story of my life 3
    Spirituality, faith and religion 4
    Setting the tone for my thoughts 5

Chapter 1 – Financial Dimension 10
    1.1 Normal planning 10
    1.2 The vagaries of planned versus actual events 12
    1.3 The virtues of detachment and discernment 12
    1.4 The roles of detachment and discernment in my retired life 15

Chapter 2 – Health and Wellbeing 17
    2.1 Introduction 17
    2.2 Physical health 18
    2.3 Mental health 19
    2.4 Spirituality 20
    2.5 Intercessory Prayer 22
    2.6 Adversity and unplanned scenarios 23

Chapter 3 – Travel 26
    3.1 Introduction 26
    3.2 Pre-planning stage 27
    3.3 Flights and accommodation 28
    3.4 Other considerations 29
    3.5 Pilgrimages 30
    3.6 Pilgrimage sites in Italy 31

Chapter 4 – Activities 34
    4.1 Introduction 34
    4.2 The PERMA Model 34
    4.3 Engagement 35
    4.4 Meaningful activities – the "M" of the PERMA Model 38
    4.5 My involvement 39

Chapter 5 – Building and Maintaining Relationships 40
    5.1 Introduction 40
    5.2 Relationships between spouses or partners 40
    5.3 Relationships between retirees and their children 48
    5.4 Relationships between retirees and their grandchildren: 49
    5.5 Retirement and friendships 50

Chapter 6 – The Gift of Nature ... 52
- 6.1 Introduction ... 52
- 6.2 Embracing nature at home ... 53
- 6.3 Forest bathing ... 54
- 6.4 Making nature part of your holiday ... 54
- 6.5 Stargazing ... 54
- 6.6 Birdwatching ... 56
- 6.7 Four-legged friends ... 56
- 6.8 Spiritual aspects of nature and the environment ... 57

Chapter 7 – Lifelong Learning ... 59
- 7.1 Introduction ... 59
- 7.2 Continuing education at school ... 61
- 7.3 Coursera ... 62
- 7.4 The University of the Third Age (U3A) ... 62
- 7.5 Virtual fitness classes, apps and eBooks ... 62
- 7.7 Enhancing spirituality in retirement ... 63

Chapter 8 – Coping with Ageing ... 65
- 8.1 Introduction ... 65
- 8.2 Living with physical limitations ... 65
- 8.3 Accepting the reality of our mortality ... 66
- 8.4 A spiritual perspective on the decline of physical capabilities in retirement ... 67

Chapter 9 – A Future Built on Hope ... 70
- 9.1 Introduction ... 70
- 9.2 Hope-filled future in Phase 1 (approximately 60 to 70 years) ... 71
- 9.3 Hope-filled future in Phase 2 (approximately 70 to 80 years) ... 73
- 9.4 Hope-filled future in Phase 3 (approximately 80 years and beyond) ... 75

Chapter 10 – Wills and Related Affairs ... 78
- 10.1 Introduction ... 78
- 10.2 Last Will and Testament ... 78
- 10.3 Enduring Power of Attorney ... 78
- 10.4 Advance Care Directive ... 79
- 10.5 Spirituality associated with end-of-life scenarios ... 81

Chapter 11 – Closing Comments ... 83
- 11.1 Motivation for writing this book ... 83
- 11.2 Post surgery, recovery and moving forward ... 84
- 11.3 The changing landscape throughout retired life ... 86

Bibliography ... 88

Endorsements

This book is a wonderful resource for pre and post-retirees to help them plan a fulfilling and enjoyable future. It succinctly elicits all the essentials required with a firm emphasis on the spiritual dimension, and is really easy reading!

Peter August (CEO Melbourne Mint, and Apostle of Divine Mercy)

You have everything in order for your transition into retirement; your finances, your travel plans and a full list of hobbies and tasks. But have you considered the spiritual dimension of your golden years? Antonio's book provides a sound, practical guide on preparing for retirement, with a critical point of difference of strengthening your relationship with God.

Simon J. Costa AO

Dr Tony Lobo has written an insightful book, an aim of which is to offer guidance to people approaching, or contemplating, retirement. The difference in this work is the infusion of spirituality as a guiding framework. I commend this book to people who want to plan constructively for their retirement, with a foundation of spirituality.

Michael Liddy (President SVDP Donvale Conference, ex-State President, St Vincent de Paul Society, Victoria)

I am a cousin of Antonio Lobo, who shared a similar upbringing, faith tradition, and outlook on life. Being over a decade younger than Tony, I have always admired his life experience and wisdom. With this same admiration, I recommend this book not only to those considering retirement or already retired but also to younger generations who may not yet be thinking about retirement. Tony's insights into retired life come from his personal experience, and his inclusion of the spiritual dimension of retirement is spot on – an important aspect that is sadly overlooked in most literature of this kind.

Ron Fernandes, Deacon, Diocese of Austin, Texas, USA.

Foreword

I have known Tony Lobo for the past two years. What I quickly gleaned was this was a man armed with a highly organised mind, powered by a very strong intellect; both of which afforded him a rich and fascinating experience in high level leadership. This combination speaks to Tony's ability to provide sage advice on achieving a happier retirement. Of even greater significance is the context in which Tony pieced this work together. It has been truly inspirational to witness Tony and his wife Anne's response to the adversity of his illness. Not knowing what the future would hold, he wrote this book at God's speed, and with an attitude of great trust in Him.

Tony's quest to provide insight into retirement through the lens of spirituality is based on his lived experience. These are not trite words of advice. They are spoken from the heart of a man who gives us a sense of the power of seeing the final chapters of our life from a spiritual perspective: that regardless of our circumstances, including inevitable trials, this is a time to flourish and to assist others to do so.

Every chapter begins with practical advice on preparing for retirement, and then expands into a discussion of the spiritual dimension. The first chapter on sound financial management, for example, flows naturally into an examination of the attitudes of discernment and detachment taught by Jesus Christ. Good stewardship is a key theme that recurs throughout the book: how God calls us to manage the gifts of money, health, friendship, and time that He has given us both in the present moment, and in the light of our future life with Him. What kind of person do we want to become as we grow older? What example of faith, wisdom, love and hope to we want to set for our children and grandchildren? What sort of a world do we want to leave to them? I believe that each and every chapter is significant, and will be of invaluable importance, because each one is intended to enlighten the mind and open the heart to thoughts of eternity.

John Canavan,
Director, Divine Mercy Publications, Australia

Introduction

Purpose of writing this book

Retirement is a stage in life into which every person will naturally have to enter. It is the culmination of our careers, and we look forward to a time of enjoyment, growth and meaning as we journey into the sunset. It is common knowledge that whilst some people transition from their working lives into a happy and fulfilling retirement, others find this transition difficult and even challenging. Many retirees experience a boost in health and happiness during the first few years after their retirement, followed by a period of declining health and unhappiness. I have reviewed a number of books and articles which purport to address issues relating to preparation for a happy retirement, which invariably discuss inter alia, finances, health and wellbeing, travel, relationships and activities. However, discussion of the spiritual dimension in retirement is conspicuously absent. Almost four years into my retirement, I am a strong proponent of the principle that the spiritual dimension should permeate and complement all the other elements mentioned previously, which contribute towards a happier retired life. My intention is to address this gap, hence this book. I shall start by citing my memoirs, which I hope will demonstrate the importance of spirituality in retirement.

A synopsis of the story of my life

I would like to begin with a brief overview of my life, which will set my memoirs in context for future deliberations. I was born in India in a Christian family. We were seven siblings and I was the eldest son. By God's grace, I was academically gifted and completed high school with flying colours. I was offered a full scholarship in a degree program. My dad, who was a government employee, was earning barely enough to make ends meet. Hence, rather than pursue a degree, I thought it would be wise to take up a career which could afford me quick access to funds, so that I could supplement my dad's wages. Jobs in the merchant navy caught my interest and fortunately I was accepted into a two-year navigation cadet's course of study. After completion of this course in 1972, I was selected by a British shipping company. At the age of nineteen, my dream came true! My dad was absolutely blown away to hear that I could provide him on a monthly basis with funds that were twice as much as he was earning. Obviously, the plight of all my siblings improved drastically, and I insisted that they all pursue university degrees of their choice. My own seafaring career progressed from cadet to third officer, second officer and then chief officer. This is when I met and married my lovely soulmate Anne; I was twenty-six and she only eighteen. I was given

command of a merchant ship at the age of twenty-eight. Anne sailed with me on most of the voyages.

After sailing as captain for a couple of years, I decided to look for shore-based opportunities, so that I could further my academic interests. At the age of thirty-one, I was offered a lecturer's position in the Maritime Academy of Malaysia. During my five-year tenure there, I completed an MBA program from a prestigious business school in the UK. I leveraged on this qualification and on my teaching experience to secure a job in the Singapore Maritime Academy. Our family (my wife, my two beautiful children and I) called Singapore home and obtained its citizenship in 1994. My goal was one day to teach in the business faculty of a prestigious university, and so I enrolled into a doctorate program. In the year 2000, I obtained my doctorate in business administration from the University of South Australia. Anne and I decided to migrate to Australia in 2001, our main objective being a change of lifestyle and opportunities for work-life balance. My initial appointment was as a lecturer in Marketing, and when I retired in 2020 I was Associate Professor of Marketing and Director of Research & Training in the business faculty of a prestigious university in Melbourne.

Spirituality, faith and religion

The *Oxford English Dictionary* defines spirituality as "The quality of being concerned with the human spirit or soul as opposed to material or physical things." According to Kees Waaijiman, the traditional meaning of spirituality is a process of re-formation that aims to recover the original shape of man, the image of God (Waaijiman 2002, p.315). To accomplish this, the re-formation is oriented toward a mould, which represents the original shape: in Judaism there is the Torah, in Christianity there is Christ, in Buddhism, Buddha and in Islam, Muhammad.

In modern times spirituality is associated with subjective experience (Saucier & Skrzypinska 2006, p.1259) and the "deepest values and meanings by which people live" (Sheldrake 2007, pp 1-2). This incorporates personal growth or transformation, usually in a context separate from organised religious institutions (Wong & Vinsky, 2009).

Faith is defined by the *Oxford English Dictionary* as "Complete trust or confidence in someone or something."

Religion is defined by the same dictionary as "The belief in and worship of a superhuman power or powers, especially a God or gods."

Setting the tone for my thoughts

There are several ideologies associated with the three elements of spirituality, faith and religion. My intention is not to delve into these in detail, nor to evaluate them critically. However, because they play a crucial role in shaping the society in which we live, I will take a moment to provide a brief overview.

As Wong and Vinsky observed, spirituality is typically viewed as a private matter, separated from the structures of organised religion. There are three main ways to view this division: some people will view spirituality more positively than religion, others will see religion as a vital source of social stability and shared moral observance, and a third group will reject both religion and spirituality in favour of agnosticism or atheism.

Australian society as a whole tends to lean more toward the view that all religious and spiritual beliefs are private matters that have no place in public debate. However, spirituality (usually referring to practices like yoga and meditation) is generally presented as a positive thing that enhances wellbeing, and is favoured over organised religion. It is a cliché, yet true, that the number of people who identify as "spiritual but not religious" has been rising ever since the social upheavals of the 1960s.

The other path of opposition to organised religion involves a rejection of the spiritual impulse in humanity — that is, atheism. It often rises from a humanistic desire to improve the lives of all human beings by natural means. Yet, in criticising religious belief and practice, it often fails to consider how many religions have acted throughout history to improve human lives by providing education, food supplies, medical care, and so

on around the world. It is my own belief that religion can be, and is, a positive force for good both for the individual believer and for the world as a whole. Even the famous atheist Richard Dawkins very recently declared himself to be a 'cultural Christian,' saying that although he 'does not believe a word of the Christian faith,' he does 'sort of feel at home in the Christian ethos' and 'would not be happy if, for example, we lost all our cathedrals and our beautiful parish churches.' (*Catholic Herald*, April 25, 2024).

This is a more nuanced position than the aggressive atheism of the early 2010s, which treated 'religion' as a vast and evil monolith to be destroyed without taking into account the vast scope of life experience, dedication, and understanding among believers in any faith tradition.

Every religion has a small group of people who will freely dedicate their entire lives to it as priests, monastics, missionaries, and so on. I would call these people the most pro-religion. At the other end of the spectrum are people who still see value in declaring themselves to be members of a particular faith, but attend religious services only on special occasions and whose prayer is mostly limited to emergencies. The majority of religious people in any tradition fall somewhere between these two poles.

These positions — anti-religion, pro-religion, and somewhat pro-religion — are the main ideologies that I see as the result of dividing religion and spirituality, and seeing them as separate and distinct.

I wish to take a rather simplistic view of these elements and would like to address them in a reverse order: Religion, faith and spirituality. By doing so, I mean to show that both faith and spirituality can flow from religious practice.

I will also state directly here that it isn't my intention to convert anyone to a particular religion, but to explore the value of religion as a whole, especially for those in later life. I am a strong advocate for inter-faith harmony and dialogue. This obviously involves contact with different religions or members of different religions. In my honest opinion, respect for all religions is of prime importance, as they provide different pathways to God. It is my view that, whichever religion one practises, there is a natural progression of faith and spirituality. If we accept Waaijiman's definition of spirituality as a process of conforming oneself to the image of God, then it follows that every religion's "mould" will shape virtues in its adherents that we can recognise by looking at the person considered the ideal human. In Jesus of Nazareth, for example, we see a profound example of wisdom, compassion, charity, and mercy. This is therefore the mould into which Christians must shape themselves, and people around them will notice whether or not they display these virtues in their daily lives. More importantly, however, in practising this religion the believer will constantly be brought to reflect on whether he or she is truly living in union with this ideal. This is the source of interior growth, the process of coming closer to God: the means by which formal religious practice develops into personal prayer and life-giving faith.

It is a common belief that the religion one follows depends in the majority of cases on where one was born and raised. It obviously depends on our childhood and early adult life, which are invariably influenced by our parents and the religion they subscribe to. I have mentioned previously that I was born in a Christian family; hence, I practise Christianity. This lays the foundation for and governs my thoughts associated with faith and spirituality.

If you believe and practise any other religion, then you might find it useful to adapt my ideas and thoughts to suit your own needs. The ways in which your religious practice translates into faith and spirituality might produce similar outcomes to those I have experienced.

Catholics of my generation may remember from catechism class that the twelve fruits of the Holy Spirit are charity, joy, peace, patience, kindness,

goodness, generosity, gentleness, faithfulness, modesty, self-control, and chastity. I chose *Happier Retirement: Grounded in Spirituality* as the title of this book because I believe that, even in this increasingly secular age, a strong and healthy spiritual practice is more important than ever for people preparing for the major life change that is the transition from paid work to retirement. In my own life, the benefits and graces have been incalculable.

It is my hope that reading this book will encourage you to meet the changes and challenges to come, not with any sense of trepidation, but with all of these wonderful fruits of the spiritual life — with charity, joy, peace, patience, and more. To reach retirement age is to have a lifetime of experience and wisdom on which to draw, and if we manage our resources (physical, financial, and emotional) with good stewardship, we have the potential for a life of great vitality and adventure ahead.

Chapter 1 – Financial Dimension

1.1 Normal planning

This is obviously one of the most important aspects in retirement, which needs to be planned for carefully. A lot of people nearing retirement are concerned that they might outlive their savings. It might be prudent for you to consult a financial planner prior to your retirement. However, in my experience, at its best this sort of financial planning provides an average ball-park monthly spending pattern in retirement. Their strategies are based on several assumptions, including longevity, intended lifestyle during retirement, overseas and domestic travel plans, lump-sum spending for one-offs like buying a new car, slush funds etc. Yet things change quite dramatically during the last third of your life, especially with respect to your health and also your likes and preferences.

The two most important financial instruments at your disposal in retirement, which you need to understand, are superannuation and government pensions. It does not take a herculean effort to get a grasp of the main rules surrounding these instruments, as copious amounts of useful information are available on dedicated websites. Details of government pensions are available at www.servicesaustralia.gov.au

The Association of Superannuation Funds of Australia (ASFA) provides estimates of how much money you will need in retirement, depending of course on your intended lifestyle. The ASFA retirement standard provides a comprehensive breakdown of expenses in retirement for either a "comfortable" or "modest" lifestyle, for couples and singles. It also estimates the minimum superannuation balance required for various scenarios during your retired life. Detailed information on the ASFA retirement standard can be found on their website: www.superannuation.asn.au

Another important aspect to consider in retirement is the home you live in. The obvious best-case scenario would be if this home is mortgage-free, and you have no other personal debts to worry about in retirement. In Australia, the primary home is excluded from calculations of assets involving pension eligibility. This home gives you a nest egg which can possibly be used later on to fund your particular needs: for example, by downsizing or obtaining a reverse mortgage.

Nowadays some people plan to work part-time during their early years of retirement. This can be motivated by the incentives of extra money, social benefits or some personal fulfilment. However, in most cases such a move invariably cannibalises the time you would want to spend on other interesting activities. Another avenue

of income for retirees is asset growth and investment returns. However, global events of the past few years have created a tough investment environment, which has caused considerable stress and anxiety to a lot of retirees.

Taking into consideration the foregoing discussion on the financial dimension, it might be prudent for you to design a budget for either a comfortable or modest lifestyle in your retirement.

1.2 The vagaries of planned versus actual events

No matter how extensive the financial planning you perform, you are bound to experience some variance between your intended scenarios and the actual situations that will arise in your retired life. Life is unpredictable in all stages of retirement, and it never follows a planned script. In retired life, you can have surprises galore, both good and not so good, in areas like health, relationships, and financial or natural disasters. There is no way of knowing what the future holds for us. Prudent planning can mitigate some of the vagaries of these events in your life. Nevertheless, you will need to be adaptable and flexible to cope with unexpected events and to find a way forward.

1.3 The virtues of detachment and discernment

All religions in some form or another advocate detachment. In Buddhism, this word essentially means freedom from lust, craving and desires. Our experiences of worldly things are evanescent: a good meal, a brand-new car or a fantastic holiday do not last forever. In Christianity, to practise detachment is "to establish and maintain a relation to everything and everybody in one's life according to which all things are valued by how much they help or hinder us in our relationship with God, the imitation of Christ, and the service of other people." (Shaw, 2016). I am not suggesting at all that we should not enjoy a great holiday or buy a new car; far from it. All I profess is that we should temper our desires and cravings in a logical manner, so as to prevent excesses.

In the words of Jesus: "Take care! Be on your guard against all kinds of greed; for one's life does not consist in the abundance of possessions." (Luke 12:15, *NRSV Catholic Edition*.) He followed these words of caution with the parable of a rich man whose harvest yielded so much grain that he decided to pull down all of his barns and build even bigger ones, complacent in his wealth and ready to "relax, eat, drink, and be merry."

"But God said to him, 'You fool! This very night your life is being demanded of you. And the things you have prepared, whose will they be?' So it is with those who store up treasures for themselves but are not rich toward God." (Luke 12:20-21.)

This is a reminder to consider our material possessions both in a pragmatic way — what are we leaving to our descendants? Are our affairs in good order, and our resources managed well so that we aren't leaving them vast quantities of unwanted items to dispose of? — and in the light of eternity. As the first canonised Australian Saint, Mary MacKillop, wrote in 1866, "Remember we are but travellers here." (Cresp, 2020). True detachment is not to treat money and possessions as an end in themselves, but to use them in harmony with God's design for a meaningful human life.

Discernment is learning to think God's thoughts after him, practically and spiritually; it means having a sense of how things look in God's eyes and seeing them in some measure "uncovered and laid bare" (Ferguson, 2023).

This means handling resources wisely and not falling into recklessness on the one hand, or timidity on the other. In the twenty-fifth chapter of Saint Matthew's Gospel, Jesus told the story of a man who went on a journey and left his money in the care of three servants. This man gave five talents (an enormous amount of money) to the first servant, two talents to the second, and one talent to the third. The first and second invested the talents wisely and doubled the amount given to them, while the third, out of fear, buried his talent in the garden until his master returned. When the first and second servants presented their master with the fruits of their good

judgement, he praised them. But he cast the third out of his house, telling him, "You ought to have invested my money with the bankers, and on my return I would have received what was my own with interest." (Matthew 25:27).

We can draw two lessons from this parable for people who are building up their savings in preparation for retirement. The first is that discernment is a good gift that God has given us, and sound financial sense is in harmony with his plan for our lives. Like the five wise bridesmaids in the parable that accompanies this one, who brought not only their lamps but enough oil to last the night, we are called to make the best use we can of the resources available to us and to ensure that we can provide for our own needs in life for as long as possible.

The second is that we do not know the day or the hour when we will come before God (represented in this story by the wealthy man) and have to give an account of all that we have done in his name. He will want to know what use we made of the resources he gave us. Have we hidden our talents out of fear that we will not be enough, or have we worked and invested sensibly to provide for ourselves and those in our care, and then looked outward from there to use our resources for the good of the world?

1.4 The roles of detachment and discernment in my retired life

I shall now illustrate the role that these virtues have played in the financial dimension of my retired life. Prior to retirement, I had budgeted a significant lump sum for the purchase of an electric vehicle (EV) to replace my ten-year-old car. I spent considerable time and effort researching the benefits of an electric vehicle, and I really fancied owning one. However, when I retired my mechanic advised me that my car was in impeccable condition and it had done very low mileage. He also assured me that he could take care of it for at least the next ten years. After some thought and logical reasoning that after all a car is essentially a means of transport, I decided to shelve my earlier plan to purchase an electric vehicle. This decision afforded me a large slush fund, which I could then allocate towards paying for something more meaningful and beneficial in my retired life.

Another, similar example is related to an asset that I owned pre-retirement. I had purchased this asset with a view to taking advantage of negative gearing and also for its prospective capital appreciation. After retirement, however, I was being unnecessarily hassled with maintenance and tenancy issues. My friends advised me to retain this asset as it would appreciate in value over the years, but guided by the virtue of discernment, I decided to liquidate this asset and reallocate the funds into our superannuation. This decision relieved me of an unnecessary mental burden.

The first of these decisions conserved money that I already had, and the second made more money available to me in a usable form. Letting go of the things I wanted but didn't really need — an electric car, and an asset that I hoped would bring me good returns in the future — required me to think about what I really valued, and what I wanted to achieve with the resources I had. Ultimately, everything we have is a gift from God, and money, like everything else, is a means to live according to his plan for us. Detachment is not about hollowing ourselves out and denying ourselves the joys of life, but becoming empty and still enough to receive more from God and listen to his word in our daily lives.

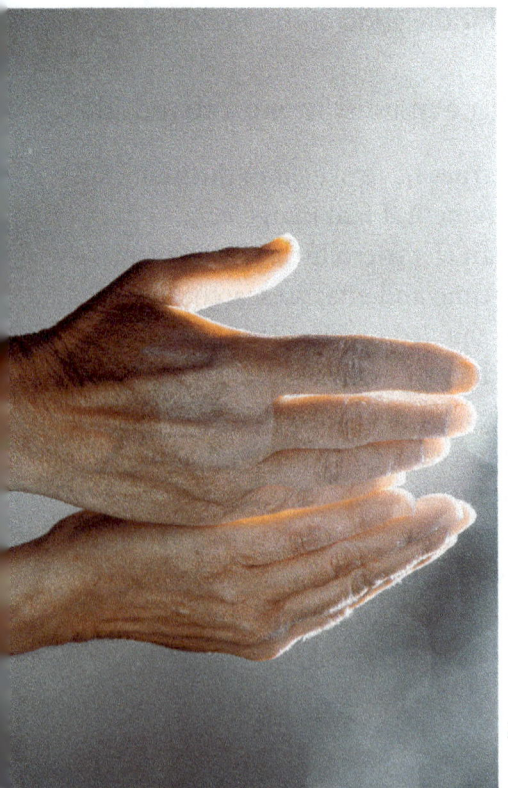

And discernment is the gift of knowing when to conserve and when to let go. In this way, we can be good stewards of everything that God has placed in our care, both now and for the rest of our lives.

'Well done… (since) you have been trustworthy in a few things, I will put you in charge of many things; enter into the joy of your master.' (Matthew 25:21.)

Chapter 2 – Health and Wellbeing

2.1 Introduction

Erik Erikson is well known for his theory on the psychosocial development of human beings. He categorises eight stages of psychosocial development commencing with infancy and ending with late adulthood. This final stage begins at the age of 65 and lasts throughout the rest of your life (Cherry, 2023).

Erikson defines this as a time of transition when people tend to look retrospectively over what they have created and produced and what legacy they might leave behind. However, if people do not feel a sense of accomplishment when they look back at their lives, then they may fall into despair and focus more on regrets (ibid.) I wish to address the importance of health and wellbeing associated with the stage of late adulthood (which is essentially the same as your retired life) in the areas of physical health, mental health and spirituality.

2.2 Physical health

This is obviously contingent on our diet and lifestyle, which includes regular exercise. A balanced diet provides nutrients like proteins, complex carbohydrates and healthy fats. We should consume fresh rather than processed foods, and additionally, we should not overeat. We would benefit from reducing our meat consumption and replacing some of it with fresh plant-based foods. The Mediterranean diet, which includes vegetables, fruit, herbs, nuts, whole grains, moderate amounts of dairy, poultry, eggs, seafood and healthy oils like olive oil, has been shown to be one good option (HealthDirect, 2024).

We should endeavour to reduce our intake of sugar and salt as these can contribute directly or indirectly to a host of illnesses. We need to drink adequate amounts of water and always stay hydrated. It is a good practice to have your water bottle to hand. Finally, we need to be cognisant of the many risks of alcohol and the benefits of reducing its consumption. So far we have discussed what to eat and drink to stay healthy, but paradoxically there are several proven benefits of fasting, especially intermittent fasting. However, you might want to consult your medical practitioner prior to undertaking any type of fasting.

Physical exercise is particularly important in our retired lives. It helps with our cardiovascular health, muscular strength and bone density. The World Health Organisation (WHO) provides guidelines for recommended physical activity for people of all ages, which can be found on their website at https://www.who.int

Some forms of physical activity include walking, dancing, swimming, regular workouts in a gym, and other sports. Physical activity can be fun and social and it contributes towards your mental health, which is discussed in the next section.

2.3 Mental health

According to the World Health Organization, mental health is "a state of mental well-being that enables people to cope with the stresses of life, realize their abilities, learn and work well, and contribute to their community. It is an integral component of health and wellbeing that underpins our individual and collective abilities to make decisions, build relationships and shape the world we live in." (WHO, 2022.)

The classical Latin phrase "*Mens sana in corpore sano*" translates to the cliché we all know, "a healthy mind in a healthy body." This is why, as discussed in the previous section, physical activity is an essential aspect of and precursor to maintaining mental health. Other elements which contribute towards mental health are sleep, smiling, keeping calm, and spirituality. I wish to discuss these elements briefly.

The Sleep Foundation talks about the salient features of sleep on its website, https://www.sleepfoundation.org

During sleep, the brain works to evaluate and remember thoughts and memories. Lack of sleep is therefore especially harmful to the consolidation of positive emotional content. This can influence mood and emotional reactivity and is tied to the development and severity of mental health disorders.

Smiling increases mood-enhancing hormones while decreasing stress-enhancing hormones, including cortisol and adrenaline. It also reduces overall blood pressure. "And because you typically smile when you're happy, the muscles used trigger your brain to produce more endorphins – the chemical that relieves pain and stress." (Walden University, 2024).

Keeping calm is synonymous with mindfulness, which is "the basic human ability to be fully present, aware of where we are and what we're doing, and not overly reactive or overwhelmed by what's going on around us." (Mindful, 2020).

Mindfulness is not something we need to set aside a specific time to do, but instead something that we can integrate into our daily lives. If you are eating, are you thinking about other things and wolfing down the food without tasting it, or are you aware of the flavours and taking a moment to enjoy what you eat? If you are getting ready for bed, are you distracted by technology, or are you focused on becoming quiet and comfortable, ready to fall asleep? Of course, sometimes we simply have to act quickly and get things done. Even then, however, we will do a better job if we are fully present physically and mentally instead of having half of our minds somewhere else.

Some activities which contribute towards mindfulness include cooking, gardening, participating in sport, arts and crafts, or learning a new language. All of these processes help us to become aware of our bodies and minds, and therefore to become more present in the moment as we work. The other very important contributor to mindfulness is spirituality, which I shall discuss in the next section.

2.4 Spirituality

There are varied and differing views about spirituality. My position, as stated at the outset of this book, is that faith and spirituality flow from religious practice.

Prayer is central to any religion. In Catholicism, there are three forms of prayer: vocal prayer, meditation and contemplation. As Sr. John Dominic Rasmussen, OP, explains:

- **Vocal prayer** "speaks to God, whether by mental or spoken words."
- **Meditation** "seeks to understand what God has revealed and to allow the beauty of His truth to move our hearts, so that we can understand and respond to what He asks of us."

- **Contemplation** "is a gift of God and a gaze of faith that abides in union with Christ… (it) tends to be the form that requires the most patience and receptivity on our part, as we need to be willing to patiently wait for His gift." (Rasmussen, 2023).

There is no right or wrong way to pray, as long as God is at the centre. "All prayer is a raising of the heart to God," writes Louis St. Hilaire, "but every believer responds to God's invitation differently, so this raising of the heart can be expressed in many ways." (St Paul Center for Biblical Theology, 2019). Some people are naturally drawn to solitary, meditative prayer, while others find it easier to pray as part of a group. Some people love silence, while others opt for music or recordings to help them concentrate. Retirement from full-time work can give you more time to explore which methods of prayer bring you closest to God. This has certainly been the case for me. Each day, I set aside a brief period in which to make an examination of conscience, going over how I have served God that day and what I need to do better in areas where I have fallen short. In the previous chapter, I wrote about making good use of God's gifts of material resources, and the same thing goes for his gift of time. Do we spend the hours of each day well, in ways that are healthy for our bodies, minds, and spirits?

Prayer is something that enriches our lives. The Rosary, which I say each day with my family, is both a vocal and meditative form of prayer: we speak the words, and this gives a structure to our inner meditations on the life of Christ. In this way, religion (in the form of sacred words written down thousands of years ago, and used formally in worship) flows into spirituality, which brings us closer to the heart of God.

Vocal and mental prayer are things that we do, opening up a dialogue between ourselves and God. We praise him and ask him to provide for the needs of our lives, and he gives us the graces we need to deal with our daily challenges. Contemplation is something different: a one-way flow of inspiration and love from God to us. For me, this takes place each week in Holy Adoration, when I sit for an hour before the Eucharist. I simply stay in the church and gaze at Jesus, and allow him to gaze at me. This is what we will do in heaven, and it is a gift from him to be able to do it here on earth as well.

2.5 Intercessory Prayer

Finally, I wish to highlight the power of intercessory prayer. Through this type of prayer "we bring someone else's needs before God, trusting Him to take care of others, whether they are loved ones, friends, enemies or total strangers. Praying for the living and the dead is one of the Spiritual Works of Mercy." (Szyszkiewicz, 2023).

For retirees, this is an important contribution that we can make to the lives of those around us, especially our families. A lifetime in the workforce will have taught us that no matter how skilled or efficient we are, we can't do everything: we can't fix every problem, but we can join with others and do our part to make things better. It is the same way with prayer. We can't solve all the problems that our children will face as they grow up, but we can join our prayers for them with the powerful prayers of the entire Church, and trust that God will hear and answer according to his will.

For those who have become too frail to work outside the home anymore, whether through age or illness, this way of holding the needs of the world in their hearts and offering them up to God is a wonderful, powerful gift that they can still offer. Loneliness is a real fear for people who realise that they and their loved ones are growing old, but prayer will always give us a share in the life of the Church, both to pray for others and to receive their prayers for us in turn.

Szyszkiewicz also mentions praying for enemies, which is something that Jesus has told us to do (Matthew 5:44). This is much harder than praying for those we love, of course. But as we enter the third age of our lives, the final stage of psychosocial development described by Erikson, and look back on what we have done with the decades that came before, coming to a place of peace and acceptance where we can pray for those who have hurt us instead of wishing them ill can be an important part of making peace with our lives and resolving the pain of the past.

2.6 Adversity and unplanned scenarios

The *Collins Dictionary* defines adversity as "a very difficult or unfavourable situation," synonymous with hardship, trouble, distress and suffering.

I am certain that you can recount one or more incidents in your life which completely shattered your hopes and aspirations, or worse still, almost caused a fatality. One such incident that haunts me even today occurred on my first voyage as master of a very old merchant navy cargo ship. We encountered extremely severe weather on the Japanese sea coast. Anne and my five-month-old son were on board the ship. We received an SOS message from a ship sinking in our vicinity, but couldn't assist as we ourselves were in grave danger of foundering. By God's grace, we somehow limped to the nearest "port of refuge." We learnt later on that all the crew of the sinking ship were fortunately rescued by the Japanese Coast Guard. I recall that although I prayed then, my faith and spirituality were lukewarm. This possibly caused me considerable stress and anxiety.

In the three years since my retirement, Anne has consistently endeavoured to strengthen my faith, without which we certainly couldn't have coped during the recent adversity which has unexpectedly shattered our lives.

For the past 15 years or so, I have paid particular attention to my physical and mental health. As we love to travel, I had made a commitment after retirement to do as many overseas trips as we could financially and physically afford. In mid-2023, we commenced planning for a five-week tour of Europe in the month of March 2024. Our intention was to visit family in France and then travel to pilgrimage sites in Italy, Croatia, Switzerland and Turkey. A week before our trip, I mentioned to Anne that I was feeling the best I'd ever been, physically, mentally and spiritually.

We were flying from Melbourne to Geneva, with a one-night transit stop in Singapore. After arriving at Singapore on March 13th, we did a little bit of shopping and then indulged in the local cuisine. Towards evening, Anne noticed a yellowish tint in my eyes. She sneaked this information to my daughter who is a medical practitioner in Melbourne. Her obvious advice was to check my urine, which was also yellowish. I put this down to dehydration and said that I would drink copious amounts of water to clear my system. Mentally, I was on a high and looking forward to reaching Europe. However, my daughter advised me to do an urgent blood test and if it was clear, I could proceed to Geneva the next day.

It was now about 9 pm, and all the clinics were shut. Anne and I attended an after-hours hospital to perform the blood test. On March 14th at 8am we were advised that all my liver function indicators were astronomically high. This was despite the fact that all these indicators were perfectly normal in the routine test I had undertaken just four months prior. We cut short our trip and took the earliest flight back home to Melbourne. Just hours after our arrival on the morning of March 15th, I underwent extensive CT scans, MRIs and ultrasounds. At 4pm, the surgeon called me and gave me this life-shattering one liner: "I am sorry to tell you that you have pancreatic cancer."

Our entire world fell apart! Anne and I just held our hands together and prayed to our God to give us the strength and fortitude to see us through this unexpected ordeal. This is when our religion, faith and spirituality came to the fore and comforted us. No amount of money or any other worldly benefits could ever have afforded us the gift of calmness, serenity and rational thinking that we experienced. We surrendered ourselves entirely to our God and quietly uttered the phrase, "Thy will be done."

Since then, I have followed all the expert medical advice, and underwent major surgery on April 19th. I shall discuss the post-surgery and recovery phase in Chapter 11. This monumental adversity has affirmed in us the very important role that religion, faith and spirituality play in our lives, especially after retirement.

Chapter 3 – Travel

3.1 Introduction

I am sure that you, like the majority of retirees, have dreamt of having the freedom to travel in your retirement. You won't need to worry about building short holidays around your working life, or returning to your office or workplace to find heaps of paperwork or an endless string of emails to attend to.

Travel opens our minds to things we have never experienced or seen before. We meet people of different nationalities and get the opportunity to soak in their culture and lifestyle. Our most cherished memories and exhilarating experiences are often linked to our travels.

There are different types of holidays depending on our preferences and, obviously, state of health. As a general rule, people in their early retirement years (say 60 to 70) aspire to embark on active travel, for example hiking, snorkelling, white water rafting or parasailing. In later years (say 70 to 80) people generally prefer organised trips where they are essentially passive watchers and listeners. Finally, after 80 people generally opt to travel closer to home.

Anne and I are avid travellers, having first experienced visits to many global port cities during my tour of duty as a merchant navy officer. During our shore-based working lives, we made a conscious effort to travel as a family to at least one new destination on each trip, including cities in the US, Canada, Europe, South America, New Zealand, South East Asia and China. After our retirement, the zeal for travel was only exacerbated, and so we have travelled extensively during the past 4 years. We are glad to share our advice and practical tips to make your travel affordable, enjoyable and memorable.

3.2 Pre-planning stage

This is the most important stage, when you need to do extensive and targeted research on your chosen destination and the cities you plan to visit. The internet provides an information highway, but you need to be efficient and selective about the websites you read. In our experience, authentic reviews posted on TripAdvisor and TravelVlogs have been quite handy in helping us get an overview of the cities we had in mind to visit. If you have friends or relatives who have recently travelled to those destinations, then they would certainly be a great source of information as well. If you have decided to join an organised tour group which arranges all your travel (including flights, accommodation and tour guides) for a lump-sum amount, then you are in luck: we have ventured previously on several of these organised tour groups, and found them great fun as we invariably met lovely like-minded travellers. However, the downside is that the itinerary is generally rigid and most tours cover several cities in a short period of time. In the past 5 years or so, we have not subscribed to tour groups, as we like to stay put in one city and soak in the environment for a longer period of time.

3.3 Flights and accommodation

We next lock in our main international flights, generally 6 to 8 months prior to our travel. If possible, we travel during the off-peak or shoulder periods, although this is not always feasible owing to the vagaries of seasonal weather patterns. We compare the price of air tickets using a third-party website, for example Skyscanner, Expedia or Webjet etc. However, we never book our tickets through a third-party provider as there are several limitations. Any cancellations or changes to flights have to made by the third party, and this may be cumbersome at times. Using the price points which we have obtained from third-party providers, we then endeavour to book our flights online directly with particular airlines. Besides the cost of the air tickets, we pay particular attention to the duration of the flight, number of stopovers, and costs associated with cancellation and change of flights. Our preference is to obtain a refund upon cancellation and not be burdened by receiving credit vouchers for future travel with that airline.

The next thing to book is accommodation. For us the most important aspect is the location. For example, if we are travelling by train inter-city in Europe, we would prefer to choose accommodation near the main railway terminus. This is usually also close to the city centre. The airports are generally quite distant from the city centre, and sometimes the cost of transfer from the airport to the hotel can be exorbitant. We have used Airbnb, booking.com and hotelscombined.com extensively; however, there are also several other accommodation providers. The important thing is to endeavour not to pre-pay, but instead to pay at the destination or very close to the date of occupation. Also, please ensure that you obtain free cancellation until almost the date of your intended stay.

3.4 Other considerations

I shall briefly address some other strategies to make your travel seamless, stress-free and fulfilling. You will certainly benefit considerably from packing light and by downsizing on your checked baggage. Learn a few words or phrases of the local language and keep Google Translate ready at hand. Once you reach your destination, endeavour to book half- or full-day tours to places of interest. If you wish you can also do this ahead of time by booking online with providers like Viator or Intrepid. We have learnt that Trainline is an excellent resource for booking inter-city trains in Europe. Also, domestic flights in Europe are quite cheap when booked in advance with budget airlines

like Ryanair, Vueling or EasyJet. The public transport in most developed countries is cost-effective and easy to use. The hop-on/hop-off bus is a great alternative for getting around. Travel insurance is a must, and you might even be entitled to free insurance from the provider of your credit card. However, please read the fine print of this insurance, and check the level of cover provided, especially medical cover. You would be well advised to check Smart Traveller for rules governing visas, entry and exit requirements, health and security.

We have addressed the essentials of travel, which obviously play an important role in enhancing our physical and mental health. I shall now discuss how to grow spiritually during our travel, which involves mixing and matching pilgrimage sites with those of leisure.

3.5 Pilgrimages

"In general, a pilgrimage is a journey to a sacred place in order to experience a personal transformation… Some take the journey to demonstrate religious devotion, while others go to learn about historically significant spiritual events that have taken place at specific destinations." (Youth Voices, 2020).

In our past 8 years of travel, Anne and I have intentionally built in places of pilgrimage near the cities that we visit as part of our travel itinerary. The graces that we have received in doing so have been immeasurable, together with the transformation of our spiritual being. I would like to mention some of these sites, which Christians and others generally visit in droves.

The Holy Land is the birthplace of Christianity, and a visit to the sacred places therein brings the Bible to life and enables you to walk in the footsteps of Jesus Christ. The main sites on this tour would be Cana, Nazareth, the Sea of Galilee,

Capernaum, the Jordan River, Bethany, the Mount of Olives and Garden of Gethsemane, the Dead Sea, the Wailing Wall, the Temple Mount, Golgotha and the Garden Tomb. For us the greatest gift was the understanding and visualisation of how the Scriptures were fulfilled and the strong nexus between the Old and New Testaments. We definitely recommend that you book a tour package with the several operators available, which include the provision of local guides and a spiritual director.

3.6 Pilgrimage sites in Italy

Rome: this is the capital city of Italy and also of the Lazio region. Some of the important pilgrimage sites are St. Peter's Basilica, Saint John Lateran, the Sistine Chapel, and the Scala Sancta (the Holy Stairs). You might also want to avail yourself of a Papal audience, the date and time of which is published by the Vatican on the official Papal audience website.

From Rome you can travel by train to Assisi to visit the Basilica of St. Francis, the Basilica of St. Clare and the tomb of Blessed Carlo Acutis.

Lanciano: this an ancient Roman town in Italy, where "the first recognized and perhaps greatest miracle of the Eucharist" took place in the 8th century A.D. (Bergeron, 2024). The Eucharist is the source and summit of the Christian life, and it is the greatest sacrament available to Catholics. For myself, every time I attend Holy Mass, I am reminded of the miracle at Lanciano during the consecration of the Host.

Loreto: Set in the hills of central Italy, the town of Loreto is "famed throughout the world for the Holy House of the Virgin Mary of Nazareth." (Thoman, 2022). According to local tradition, the Annunciation took place here in this small house, which "consists of three walls of stacked stones." (ibid.)

Tradition holds that the Holy House was brought to Loreto 'by the angels' in the thirteenth century. Despite the modern theory that this refers to a family with the surname 'Angeli,' Catholics have always respected and loved the much older story of its miraculous translation from the Holy Land to Loreto by the angels of God (Dufaur, 2016).

Whilst in Venice, you can take a local train and visit the Basilica of St. Anthony of Padua.

If you happen to be in Milan, you can take a one-hour train ride to Turin to visit the Chapel of the Holy Shroud.

Santa Maria delle Grazie Church in San Giovanni Rotondo, where Padre Pio spent most of his life, has become a well-known pilgrimage site since his death in 1968.

The following Marian pilgrimage sites draw millions of people to them every year:

- The Sanctuary of Our Lady of Lourdes in France. You can travel from Paris to Lourdes by train, which takes approximately 5 hours. Alternatively, you can take a domestic flight from Paris to Tarbes, which is the airport in Lourdes.
- The Sanctuary of Our Lady of the Rosary of Fatima is an important Marian shrine. It is only an hour's ride from Lisbon to Fatima on the train, or about an hour and half by road.
- The Basilica of Our Lady of Guadalupe is located in Mexico City, Mexico. The Virgin of Guadalupe is considered the Patroness of Mexico and the Continental Americas.
- The Church of St. James in Medjugorje. Here you will experience one of the most spiritual and peaceful places on earth. You may want to experience the climb to Apparition Hill and also to Cross Mountain.
- Basilica of Our Lady of Knock, Queen of Ireland. The town of Knock is about 3 hours by train or car from Dublin.

Finally, we would recommend the Camino de Santiago, which is a series of walks that converge on Santiago de Compostela, where St. James (one of the twelve Apostles) is buried in a spectacular cathedral. People of all religions from all over the world undertake the walk, which is arguably the most popular hike on the planet. Anne and I did the Saria to Santiago walk, which covers 114 kilometres. The entire experience is absolutely unique, as we walked an average of about 20 kilometres every day. The local and foreign people we met were marvellous and friendly, and we stayed each night in a different hamlet in booked accommodation. This sort of walk contributes to all three types of health: physical, mental and spiritual.

Whether you travel as a tourist or as a pilgrim, you will find your heart, mind and spirit expanding in response to new experiences during your journeys. If you haven't travelled much during the years of your working life and now want to try it, a world of history, cuisine, language, culture, and breathtaking landscapes is about to open up to you! Once the basics like bookings, itineraries and safety precautions are put in place, you can begin to explore and challenge your own boundaries. The rewards are extraordinary!

Chapter 4 – Activities

4.1 Introduction

Positive psychology is "the scientific study of what makes life worth living" (Ackerman, 2018). Positive psychology is "a scientific approach to studying human thoughts, feelings and behaviour with a focus on strengths instead of weaknesses, building the good in life instead of repairing the bad, and taking the lives of average people up to 'great' instead of focusing solely on moving those who are struggling up to 'normal'" (Ackerman, 2018).

4.2 The PERMA Model

This is a "widely recognised and influential model in positive psychology" (Ackerman, 2018). It was developed by Martin Seligman, and published in his 2011 book *Flourish*. The acronym PERMA stands for

(a) Positive Emotion
(b) Engagement
(c) Relationships
(d) Meaning and
(e) Accomplishment.

I intend to address (a), (b) and (d) of the PERMA Model in this section on dealing with activities in your retired life, and (c) in the next section.

Positive emotions are generated when you engage in activities which bring joy into your life: for example, going on a holiday, reading a great book or enjoying a delicious meal. Admittedly, such activities are fleeting or evanescent as the joy they create is short-lived. In order for you to experience more lasting "happiness," you will need to seek out the kinds of activities associated with Engagement and Meaning. In order to do this, you will need to consider your skills and talents and possibly focus on activities that you've always wanted to do, but have been prevented from pursuing by the pressures of your working life.

4.3 Engagement

You will benefit from evaluating how you're going to spend your time and passion during retirement. Some activities that might enhance your physical, mental and spiritual health are listed below:

- Painting: this is an absorbing activity which requires focused concentration for long periods of time. You could sign up for an arts course to learn painting, or branch out into pottery, sculpture or photography. You could also visit art galleries and museums.
- Reading: if you love reading, then joining a book group or book club might interest you and help you to discover new reads. You might also want to write and publish your own book.
- Craft: you might like to create things that give you pleasure. There are ample resources available for embroidery, crochet, sewing, patchwork, card-making etc.

- Gardening: not only is this a great source of fresh air, but you can learn to grow fruits, vegetables and herbs for your own table! A beautiful garden is a source of delight, and it can support bees and native fauna which are essential for our ecosystem.
- Social clubs: these might be formal organisations like Probus, Lions, and Rotary, or local get-togethers for activities like walking, cleaning up parks or beaches, or games like chess or cards. The Community Centre in your area will be able to point you toward some of these, and local newspapers may advertise others. Or you can start your own!
- Playing in a band, singing in a choir, or other musical pursuits: if you've always wanted to learn an instrument or express yourself through singing, then this is a great time to follow up on that interest! Numerous studies have shown that music (whether you're performing it, dancing to it, or even simply listening to it) has positive cognitive and emotional effects for people of all ages, including seniors (National Center for Complementary and Integrative Health, 2022).

- Tennis, golf, ballroom dancing, and other sports: the sports that you might choose to pursue will vary according to your interests, health, location and fitness level, but all of them provide opportunities for fun, movement and social interaction. If that sounds a bit too energetic for your tastes, local Community Centres and swimming pools often have gentle exercise programs for seniors focusing on improving things like coordination, balance and flexibility as well.
- Fishing. Whether you're with a group of friends or by yourself on the riverbank or pier, this is a great way to spend time outdoors and watch the world go by. You might even catch your dinner for the day!
- Men's Shed: "Men don't talk face to face. They talk shoulder to shoulder." (The Men's Shed Association, 2024). There are now Women's Sheds and Community Sheds as well, but the primary mission of this organisation has always been to offer "a safe and friendly environment where men are able to work on their own projects… to enhance the well-being and health of their male members" (ibid.). A local Shed provides support, community, and mateship for men of all ages and backgrounds, and there are more than 1,200 such Sheds across Australia.
- Parish work in a church. Retirees are the lifeblood of any parish, acting as sacristans, catechists, and prayer group leaders among other roles, and helping with necessary tasks like cleaning, gardening, and floral arrangements for the church. Many parishes also have charity programs and connections to St Vincent de Paul conferences, which provide opportunities for volunteering with the poor and homeless. Which leads to…

4.4 Meaningful activities – the "M" of the PERMA Model

The phrase "Law of the Gift" was coined by St. John Paul II.

According to this Law, "there are two paths towards self-fulfilment and self-actualization. On the one hand we can act with self-assertion, centering and privileging our own needs and concerns. By contrast, and paradoxically, the Law of the Gift says that you become more fully human, alive and yourself to the extent that you give yourself away. You self-actualize by becoming other-focused." (Beck, 2020.) What you give will be your time, skills and resources, including money, to help someone else.

Bishop Robert Barron summarises the Law of the Gift in this way: "Your being increases in the measure that you give it away. Your being decreases in the measure that you cling to it." (Barron, 2017).

The Corporal Works of Mercy are found in the teachings of Jesus Christ and give us a model for how we should treat all others, as if they were Christ in disguise. They are "charitable actions by which we help our neighbours in their bodily needs" (*United States Catholic Catechism for Adults*, 2006, p.508).

The seven Corporal Works of Mercy are:

- Feed the hungry,
- Give drink to the thirsty,
- Shelter the homeless,
- Clothe the naked,
- Visit the sick and the prisoners,
- Bury the dead, and
- Give alms to the poor. (ibid.)

There are numerous volunteering opportunities available to you in your retirement, some of which are:

- Helping patients and providing family support in hospices and hospitals
- Working with a mental health charity
- Providing Meals on Wheels
- Assisting children with special needs
- Befriending the elderly
- Providing for the homeless.

4.5 My involvement

I joined the St. Vincent de Paul Society (Vinnies) Victoria, as a volunteer some 13 years ago. This is a Catholic lay organisation which helps people who are living in poverty, by assisting with food, clothing, furniture, utility payments, financial assistance, and giving people someone to talk to. In the State of Victoria, Vinnies have more than 250 metropolitan and regional conferences, with approximately 4000 members and associate members (all volunteers). Each conference serves a well-defined suburban area. There are welfare assistance call centres, which take calls from those who need help. Every day, in the late afternoon, the call centre sends out to the appropriate conference a list of persons (whom we call companions) who need assistance. A team comprising two volunteers then visits the home of the companion and provides whatever assistance is required. We have to deal with various scenarios including victims of domestic violence, substance abuse, homelessness, loneliness and abject poverty. Some of the children need educational support like books, school fees or laptops. I have personally found this work extremely rewarding and meaningful.

Whether your personality is more introverted or extroverted, and whether you enjoy fast-paced activities or detailed projects that take weeks or months to complete, there will be something out there for you to enjoy in your retirement. The skills and experience that you have gained across the course of your lifetime will be valuable however you choose to use them, and your community will be enriched by your contribution.

Chapter 5 – Building and Maintaining Relationships

5.1 Introduction

Retired life offers the potential for enhancing relationships between family members and friends, owing to the availability of extra time and space. However, the reality is that in some cases this may not be as attractive as envisaged, and it can present challenges for individuals and couples. A retiree may have to adjust to the lack of familiar routines and structure, and the impact on their identity as they are no longer defined by their role in the workplace. Additionally, self-esteem can be affected by the cessation of employment, which brings changes in income and perhaps status (Accord, 2024). We are all familiar with the cliché that "charity begins at home," and so I shall begin by addressing retirees' close family relationships, and later on their relationships with their friends.

5.2 Relationships between spouses or partners

Differing expectations for retirement can sometimes draw spouses apart rather than together. It is likely that they have never spent so much time together prior to one or both having retired, and they will certainly benefit if they have some common goals for retirement. (Hansen and Hass, 2015, p. 24) Both should also, where possible, have separate interests and friends of their own.

The attributes that are most beneficial in strengthening the relationship between spouses are humility, forgiveness, listening to each other and practising "give and take." As the Bible says, "Two are better than one, because they have a good reward for their toil. For if they fall, one will lift up the other; but woe to one who is alone and falls and does not have another to help." (Ecclesiastes 4:9-10.)

Some of the other secrets to a healthy relationship between spouses are:

- **Inculcate some shared interests**

You and your spouse may be proof of the saying about birds of a feather flocking together, or perhaps an example of opposites attracting. In either case, a 2015 study by the Pew Research Center found that 64% of married adults surveyed said that having shared interests was "very important" to a successful marriage (Geiger, 2016). What this looks like will vary, of course, depending on how long you've been married, whether your occupations bring you into the same social circles, and how much overlap there is between the skills and talents of both partners.

If you are newly retired, your spouse may be pleased to welcome you along to some of their regular activities, or they may wish to preserve their independence, in which case you might set out to discover entirely new activities you can take up together. The early years of retirement are a time to try things you haven't done before: you could take a painting class together, for example, or join an aquatic exercise club. You might even discover shared interests at home by borrowing new books or movies from the library and discussing them afterwards, or embarking on a joint project to develop a neglected corner of your garden.

It is also good to remember that you can enjoy seeing your spouse take pleasure in something without wanting or needing to take part in it yourself, and vice versa! (Qualls, 2021).

- **Share household chores equitably**

If "shared interests" came first on the list of things that married adults said were important for a successful marriage, then "sharing of chores" came in close behind at 56%. The division of chores during your professional years will often be based on the hours each spouse works outside the home (Geiger 2016), so a new balance will need to be found once this changes.

During our working years, when Anne was doing shift work and I had a full academic load, it took time to reach a balance of give and take that both of us were happy with. You may find, as we did, that it actually becomes easier to share chores once the pressure of work drops off. And of course, there are always external factors that influence the balance of duties between spouses; for example, when one partner is caring for elderly parents, especially if that involves travel.

While I was writing this chapter, Anne and I discussed the early influences and examples that we brought with us into our marriage, and which have shaped the way we resolve difficulties and tensions like this.

Something that has stayed with her over the years is that her parents never went to bed angry: they would always ensure they were reconciled before the day ended so that the debate didn't drag out and turn nasty, and that was a good example that she has always valued.

For me, as the eldest of seven children who helped my parents with chores and caring for younger siblings, I learned responsibility and independence at a very early age, so that was the background that I brought with me: sharing responsibility and contributing to take care of others.

It is always interesting, and fruitful, to consider what both you and your spouse bring to your relationship, what expectations you have of yourself and your partner, and how your combined skills can help you to negotiate the changes of life as a couple.

- **Be kind to each other**

This is something that sounds obvious, but it is well worth taking the time to consider concrete ways that you can act kindly in your relationship when you are suddenly spending much more time together. Clinical psychologist Dr. Lisa Firestone describes the hidden obstacles to kindness in marriage as

A) a fear of intimacy ("keeping an emotional distance… maintain(ing) old, familiar defenses that keep us feeling safe and self-protected but that actually limit us in our lives"),

B) a fantasy bond (when partners begin to "form an illusion of fusion" and then "overstep each other's boundaries," taking each other for granted), and

C) a critical inner voice (the "skewed commentary of a mean inner coach") which leads us to build cases for resentment against ourselves or our spouses. (Firestone 2016).

We may not even be aware that we are doing these things, and that is why it pays to think consciously about being kind and to work on our own personal growth in this area. In my opinion, the most important thing is to step back and avoid tit-for-tat debates, especially in cases when the argument shifts beyond the immediate issue at hand and each partner begins to bring up each other's negative points. Reading the lives of the saints provides us with wonderful examples of grace, patience and charity in close relationships with others, even when the other person may be angry or unkind. Following their lead, we can be the ones who defuse the situation, giving the other person time to calm down before coming back to work things out together.

- **Have lines of communication always open, even if one is unhappy about some aspect of the relationship**

If your spouse is expressing dissatisfaction with something that you're doing, it's easy to become defensive rather than listening. Likewise, if you are upset or angry with your spouse, there are ways that you can bring this up respectfully, and ways that are the opposite of respectful. If you have been married for a long time, you will already know the sorts of things you should definitely *not* say to your spouse if you want to keep the peace. Knowing what *to* say is harder. The transition time of retirement is a good time to reevaluate the patterns of communication that you have formed over the course of your marriage or partnership, and to work together on changing the ones that no longer serve you both.

One thing that Anne and I have found very helpful for working on communication in this way, and which we recommend to all our married friends, is a Marriage Encounter weekend. These weekends are essentially a retreat for couples: a series of talks on effective dialogue to enrich your marriage, with opportunities in between to talk over what you've learnt together "and look at yourselves and your marriage with new eyes" (Marriage Encounter Australia, 2024). They are based on a Catholic ethos, but you don't have to be Catholic to attend. You can go on a Marriage Encounter weekend at any stage in your married life, but it will be especially beneficial to take the time to discuss your lives together so far, and look toward your future as a couple, as you embark on this new phase of retired life together. In our own experience, this really helped us to open up to each other and improve the dialogue between us, and we cannot recommend it highly enough.

- **Try and be calm at all times**

What Firestone advises, first and foremost, is to "feel the feeling, but do the right thing" (2016). I think this is very sound advice. It is the mark of a mature adult to be able to acknowledge that you are angry, hurt, lonely, and so on, without using these feelings as an excuse to hurt your loved one. In effect, placing the value of the long-term relationship above the value of "winning" the argument in that moment (ibid.). This does not mean giving up your own needs or preferences, but rather, expressing these needs and preferences when both of you are calm enough to process them without overreacting emotionally.

It helps to take time to reminisce together: the positive qualities that you love in your husband or wife are more important than the flaws, and  talking often about the good times that you've shared will strengthen the bond to endure through more the difficult discussions. And paying each other compliments is important, too! We'll compliment friends, colleagues, even strangers, but we tend to assume that our spouse already knows how we feel about them, and so we let this aspect of healthy interaction slide. Tell your spouse what you like about them, and also what you love about them. Not just on special occasions, but in everyday life. The Catholic definition of love is not based on feelings, which are changeable, but "an act of the free will" that involves "choosing to 'will the good' of one's spouse in all times and circumstances" (US Conference of Catholic Bishops, 2018). For better or worse, for richer or poorer, in sickness and in health, to be a good husband or wife is to choose the course of action that will build up your spouse toward happiness and holiness; that's what it means to will the good for them. This might be in major things like making the commitment to work through a crisis in your marriage, or in small, everyday things like telling your spouse how much you enjoyed the meal they cooked that day. Any act of kindness that strengthens you both, and brings joy and life into the bond between you, captures the essence of authentic love.

- **Discuss financial matters that impact both**

Again, the financial dynamic of a relationship is unique to every partnership. You or your spouse may have been the primary breadwinner for your household, or you may have contributed equally to your shared finances throughout your working lives. One of you may be more skilled in mathematics and budgeting, and so naturally ends up doing the majority of that work, or you may sit down and do it together. No matter what balance you have struck before retirement, however, a few basic principles are necessary for a healthy relationship:

1. Ensure your financial priorities are lined up. You and your partner will probably have different ideas about the balance of saving versus spending, especially once you are no longer earning a regular salary. Working out a budget that you can both agree to will be vital, and having this system written down is also advisable. (Osteen & Neel, 2018).

2. Don't use money for leverage over your spouse. This is especially true if one of you has earnt more than the other throughout your working lives, and therefore feels more entitled to a say in how the money is spent. You are a partnership, and money needs to be shared accordingly! (Cruze, 2024.)

3. Be transparent and trustworthy. Many, many marriages have been damaged or destroyed by the sudden discovery of immense debts run up through one partner's gambling addiction, for example. Both spouses should know (or be able to find out easily) exactly how much money is available to them, where it is, and what major purchases and expenses are coming up. (Osteen & Neel, 2018).

4. Have realistic expectations. This goes hand-in-hand with setting a shared budget. Can you truly afford the house or holiday that you want? Even if the decision to buy something beyond your means is made mutually, you could be setting yourself up for years of debt, with all of the potential for conflict that this causes (Cruze, 2024.)

5. In the end, we come back to the principle of good stewardship discussed in Chapter 1. You and your spouse have shared resources at your disposal, and you both have the right (and duty) to decide together how you will use them. When these decisions are carried out with mutual respect and love, they can make a positive contribution to the overall health of a marriage. (Osteen & Neel, 2018).

- **Spend quality time with each other**

"The important thing is not what you do together; it's how you interact while doing it." (Dr. John Gottman, quoted in Qualls, 2021). If the underlying attitude is one of respect for – and delight in - your spouse's interests, talents, intelligence and humour, then the positive interactions between you as you live your lives together will be the bedrock not only of your marriage, but of your friendship.

I would like to add that the bond between Anne and me has increased tremendously after retirement owing to our common religious beliefs and faith. We use each other as sounding boards to bounce ideas and thoughts about spirituality, and we always plan and visit places of pilgrimage together. In the past 3 years, we have started a small prayer group of about 15 close friends. We meet at our place once a month to share our views about a particular aspect of spirituality, followed by fellowship. The sharing of thoughts and experiences by the participants makes for an insightful and meaningful discussion. Anne and I prepare the material for this jointly and collaboratively, and we always see things from a different angle. The process of exploring our perspectives, then researching the topics and coming back to discuss what we've found, has enriched both our faith and our bond with each other.

5.3 Relationships between retirees and their children

It is known that differences in perspectives on parenting, or any one of a range of other topics, can cause tension between parents and their adult children. Social scientists are of the view that parents need to teach their children to live within their means and to set goals for themselves. Of course parents can treat their adult children with gifts on special occasions, but these should be one-off gifts without future expectations. We have heard of some children depending financially on their parents for decades longer than they should, and taking it for granted. The acronym "KIPPERS" stands for "Kids in Parents' Pockets Eroding Retirement Savings," and it relates to adult children who are still living at home with their parents at an age when they can work and be independent (Watson, 2023).

Retirees can love their children and encourage their independence simultaneously. Some other ideas which retirees could consider in relation to their adult children are:

- Encourage them to pursue relevant tertiary or trade courses.
- Gently discuss with them a timeline for moving out of the family home. This might be a sensitive issue, but it has to be addressed.
- Bring the family together regularly on special occasions to preserve and maintain traditions and family bonds.

As you grow older, you will also need to discuss the opposite scenario with your children: what you wish to happen should you become unable to continue to live in your own home. Some retirees will opt to find an Independent Living Unit where they can be supported professionally, or to move into a residential care facility of their choice; some grown children will want their parents to live with them. It isn't an easy issue, and will require a sensible and thorough discussion ahead of time so that everyone's needs can be taken into account. There are other ways that adult children can offer support to their parents, as indeed we are instructed to do in Scripture:

"Honor your father and your mother, so that your days may be long in the land that the Lord your God is giving you." (Exodus 20:12)

"With all your heart honor your father, and do not forget the birth pangs of your mother. Remember that it was of your parents you were born; how can you repay what they have given to you?" (Sirach 7:27-28)

This involves providing mental and emotional support to elderly parents, and financial assistance if needed. Anne, who has worked in aged care, has observed that the pension by itself is often insufficient, and it is up to families to ensure that their oldest members have what they need to live with dignity.

The *United States Catholic Catechism for Adults* states that "Children owe their parents respect, gratitude, just obedience, and assistance" (p.375), and "while it is right for society to help care for the elderly, the family remains the rightful source of support" (ibid.).

5.4 Relationships between retirees and their grandchildren:

"Grandchildren are the crown of the aged, and the glory of children is their parents." (Proverbs 17:6)

This bond can demonstrate unconditional love and it can be one of the most satisfying things in the life of retirees. If they are heavily involved in their grandchildren's lives, there is a natural flow-on effect in the enhancement of bonding and respect with their own children. However, sometimes grandparents might feel imposed upon or taken for granted if too much is expected from them in the way of childcare. Some of the things that retirees could do with their grandchildren are:

- Read to them and perhaps accompany them to the local library
- Take them to a show, park or zoo

- Build Lego and models together
- Indulge in painting with them
- Organise a treasure hunt
- Help them with their school project
- Tell them stories of their own childhood and upbringing.

As I noted briefly above, disagreements can arise if adult children choose to raise their own offspring in a way that differs from that of their parents. This is a challenging and often painful matter, but I believe that it will often be counter-effective to interfere, and may even create a rebellious relationship between the generations. If asked, of course, I would always tell my children what I believed, especially where the faith was concerned, but I wouldn't step in without invitation. As with other areas in which your children's lifestyle may be different from your own, it can be good to give subtle advice and guidance, but not to try and force change; they are adults, and have the right to their own lives and decisions.

5.5 Retirement and friendships

One of the key requirements of a happy life in retirement is to have good friends, as they provide emotional support and contribute to our overall wellbeing. The two priorities in friendship during this period are: first, sustaining and deepening our most important long-term friendships; and second, reaching out and embracing new friends. Jeff Gill gives the following advice in an article in *Business Investor* (Gill, 2024):

- Reignite old flames by dusting off phone numbers, organising reunions and exploring social media;
- Forge new paths by joining clubs and activities, taking a class or workshop or by becoming a community volunteer;
- Embrace technology by making video calls, engaging in online games and communities and social media groups.

The overarching message is Quality over Quantity. The friendships we cultivate will stand us in good stead throughout our retirement, and give a deeper meaning to our later years.

If you're reading this book to help you plan a fulfilling retirement, I believe it's safe to assume that you aren't planning to hop onto your deathbed just yet! However, it's a useful mental exercise to imagine what we would think and feel at the very end of our lives, and then use what we learn from that to plan for the years ahead.

According to the Australian palliative caregiver Bronnie Ware, these are the top five wishes expressed by the dying:

1) "I wish I'd had the courage to live a life true to myself, not the life others expected of me."
2) "I wish I hadn't worked so hard."
3) "I wish I'd had the courage to express my feelings."
4) "I wish I had stayed in touch with my friends."
5) "I wish I had let myself be happier" (Ware 2012, p. v).

Human relationships, especially the bonds with family and close friends, are at the core of who we are as people. Despite the challenges and struggles, it is worth making the time to be among those we love, and to strengthen the ties of mutual support and kindness as we age.

> *"Even to your old age I am he,*
> *even when you turn gray I will carry you.*
> *I have made, and I will bear;*
> *I will carry and will save."*
>
> **Isaiah 46:4**

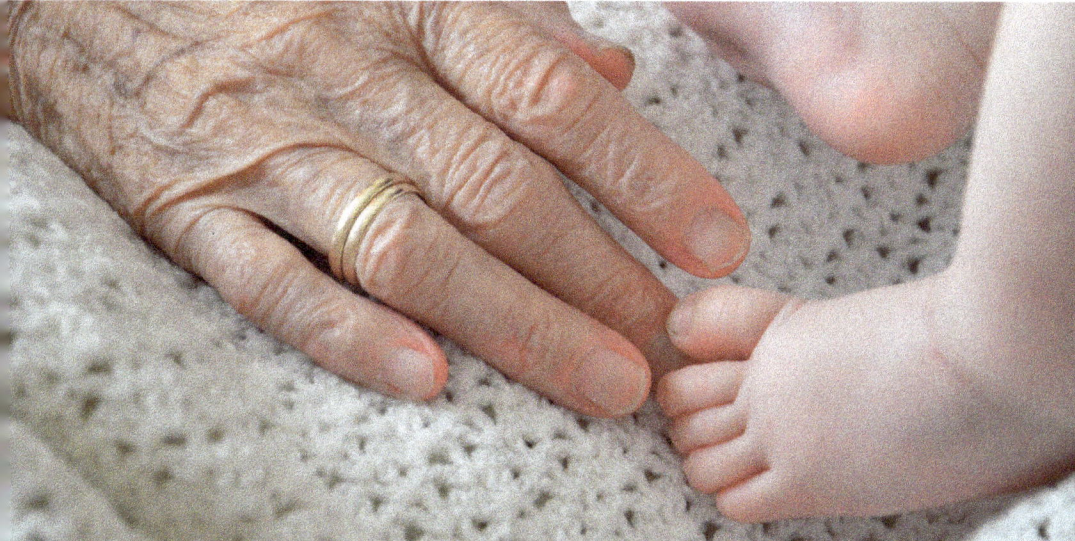

Chapter 6 – The Gift of Nature

6.1 Introduction

Retired life presents an opportunity to scale back on busyness and make some time for yourself. You can now accept life at a pace that is reasonable and pursue activities that interest you. The American Psychological Association (APA) recommends spending time in the great outdoors, which can improve your mental health, combat stress and help you see the brighter side of life (Weir, 2020). Connecting with nature can be as simple and easy as spending time a park, nature reserve, forest or beach. The APA lists the following mental health benefits of spending time in nature:

- Improved cognitive function,
- Enhanced memory and attention control,
- Lowered stress levels,
- Better social skills, and
- Protection against depression and anxiety. (ibid.)

One 2015 study found that participants who spent forty minutes walking in a natural environment reported more emotional and cognitive benefits than those who walked for a similar amount of time in an urban environment

(Quoted in Jiminez et al., 2021). Spending time in the natural world helps to overcome mental fatigue, and it activates the parasympathetic nervous system, which helps in relaxation (Jiminez et al. 2021).

The biophilia hypothesis, defined by *Encyclopaedia Britannica* as the "idea that humans possess an innate tendency to seek connections with nature and other forms of life" (Rogers, 2023), is one explanation for this powerful draw that the natural world exerts over us, and for the positive benefits of immersing ourselves in nature. Our indoor, technology-based lives are very different from those of our ancestors, whose existence was far more closely tied to the land and the changing of the seasons (Rogers, 2023): it makes sense that we still feel that connection. Even watching a *video* of the natural world has been shown to have a beneficial emotional and cognitive effect, although not as much as actually going outside, of course! (Weir, 2020).

It does not matter whether you perform activities in natural settings on a daily basis, or whether you consolidate them into a weekly binge: the accrued health benefits are just the same. Here are some ideas and activities that you can participate in throughout your retirement to connect with nature, based on a list from *The Retirement Handbook* by Ted Heybridge (2021, pp.70, 80, 148).

6.2 Embracing nature at home

Consider walking short distances rather than taking the car. You might also want to plan your driving route so that you can swap busy roads for green spaces. Make use of any walking trails close to your home, taking a stroll in a park or on a nearby beach. People come from all over the world

to see our beautiful Australian landscapes as well as our unique flora and fauna, and we have them right here on our own doorsteps! From the eucalypts, wattle trees and banksias growing in your local park to the native birds you can attract to your backyard feeder (more on that shortly), you can always find a way to enjoy the rich natural resources available all around us, and experience the benefits to your physical, mental and spiritual health.

6.3 Forest bathing

The Japan National Tourism Organization defines forest bathing, or *shinrin-yoku*, as a "simple and therapeutic act of spending time in a forest."

> Take a moment to appreciate your surroundings and listen to the sounds around you: twittering birds, rustling bush, trickling streams. Breathe in clean, fragrant air and soak in the sights of the textured ground and the shapes of the leaves in the sky. Touch the soft, green moss carpeting the shaded stones, or the rough bark on the trees. Let the stillness around you influence your state of mind and make you forget the constant motion of the city. (2024).

One way of indulging in forest bathing is to rent a cabin in a nature reserve or in a caravan park.

6.4 Making nature part of your holiday

There are numerous walking holidays available globally: just pack your walking gear and soak up the fresh air and scenery. Ecotourism is a defined as "responsible travel to natural areas that conserves the environment, sustains the well-being of the local people and involves interpretation and education" (The International Ecotourism Society, 2006).

6.5 Stargazing

Everyone can enjoy astronomy simply by stepping outside on a clear night. The Canadian Space Agency gives the following tips:

- Move away from city lights;
- Find a clear spot where you can see as close to the horizon as possible;
- Check the weather forecast;
- Get in touch with your nearest astronomy club.

(The Canadian Space Agency, 2021.)

Many of the night sky's beautiful sights, such as constellations and the Milky Way, can be enjoyed with the naked eye. This includes our own Southern Cross! Sky maps and star finders can help guide you by pointing out the location of celestial objects. You can also use apps like Stellarium to turn your smartphone into an interactive star finder.

Gazing up at the vastness of the night sky can be a profoundly spiritual experience in itself, as the Psalmist showed around three thousand years ago:

> *When I look at your heavens, the work of your fingers,*
> *the moon and the stars that you have established;*
> *what are human beings that you are mindful of them,*
> *mortals that you care for them?*
>
> **(Psalm 8)**

6.6 Birdwatching

Sharon Stiteler, the founder of Birdchick.com, writes that many types of birds hang out in backyards, especially if you have bird feeders. She advises you to fill up the feeders with birdseed – black oil sunflower seed is a good overall choice – and then sit back and see how many different species show up. A fountain or shallow bird bath where birds can bathe and drink might make your yard an even more popular place, although please ensure that you take precautions to prevent cats from climbing it. The best way to birdwatch is to look and listen, because many birds have unique songs and calls. A bird book can be very helpful for identifying them.

There are many other activities you can use to connect with nature, including:

- Volunteering to work on an environmental or conservation project to protect species, or to address biodiversity;
- Indulging a passion for wild flowers;
- Foraging (with caution – please be especially careful with mushrooms!)
- Kayaking

Time outdoors can be divided broadly into two categories: active (biking, jogging, swimming etc) and passive (having a cup of tea on the porch, reading on the beach, or simply sitting quietly and breathing in the fresh air). (Jiminez et al., 2021.)

How you choose to balance these will depend on your interests and fitness level, but all of them will help you to feel more calm, centred, and happy if you engage in them regularly. You might even find that you're drawn to prayer as you walk or sit in the great outdoors!

6.7 Four-legged friends

There are many reasons why dogs are known as man's best friend: they provide companionship in retirement and smother you with unconditional love. They get you out for daily walks, which will help with your fitness and social needs, and allow you to connect with nature. Overall, dogs give far more to your life than they take.

6.8 Spiritual aspects of nature and the environment

Caritas Australia states that "The earth and all life on it are part of God's creation. We are called to respect this gift. We are responsible for taking care of the world we live in and for sharing all the wonders and resources the earth gives us." (Caritas Australia, 2022).

Saint Francis of Assisi reminds us that our common home is "like a sister with whom we share our life and a beautiful mother who opens her arms to embrace us." He goes on to say, "Praise be to you, my Lord, through our Sister, Mother Earth, who sustains and governs us, and who produces various fruit with coloured flowers and herbs."

We need to understand not only the value the Catholic Church places on care for our common home, this planet, but also how inseparable the bond is between concern for nature, justice for the poor, commitment to society and interior peace. Pope John Paul II used the word *conversion* to describe the shift in mindset necessary to halt the destruction of the earth. This word, with its religious overtones, suggests a way forward: a deep change of heart, and the adoption of a global attitude of respect for God's creation, both human and non-human.

In the chapter about finance, I discussed the inheritance that we will leave to our children and grandchildren, and wrote about the importance of good stewardship of our resources. This inheritance is not only financial, but ecological: are we working to leave them a beautiful, healthy world for them to live in? We can play our part by recycling and reducing waste, by planting trees and volunteering in efforts to clean up our natural spaces, and by walking or taking public transport when possible instead of driving. We can also sign (or start!) petitions at a local, state and federal level to make our voices heard for the protection of our planet.

Our world is beautiful, and filled with natural riches that shape, comfort and heal us the more we engage with them. There are so many ways we can benefit from spending time in nature, and many of these involve giving something back as well – helping, cleaning, growing, feeding wildlife, and working for change. As retirees, we are the elders of our community, and we have a duty to lead by example in treating our earth sustainably and well. We want our planet to bless our great-great-grandchildren with the gifts of God, just as it blesses us!

Chapter 7 – Lifelong Learning

7.1 Introduction

In your retired life you may have developed a yearning to devote yourself to a new challenge. This might present itself in the form of learning a new subject, a new language or a new skill; something you've always been prevented from doing because of time or financial constraints during your working life. Signing up to such a challenge might help to give some structure to your day or week, where you set aside a few hours to learn something new. Lifelong learning is good for the brain, for mental well-being, and for enhancing self-esteem. An American advisory service for seniors (Senior Lifestyle, 2024a) suggests that lifelong learning benefits retirees in the following areas:

- **Adaptability and empowerment.**

   Do you know how to pay your bills online, or to transfer money from one account to another in an instant if you need to? Can you browse websites to get the best quote for maintenance on your house or car? Are you up to date with your knowledge of scams targeting seniors, which cost Australians over 65 more than $120.7 million in 2022 alone? (Kollmorgen, 2023).

If you want to sign online petitions or contact politicians by email over issues that you care about, or design and print a flyer to raise awareness in your neighbourhood, can you do so? Staying on top of constantly-changing technology can be a challenge, even for early adopters who have been using home computers since the 80s and 90s, but the benefits of using it to support your lifestyle are immense and empowering.

- **Enhanced self-esteem and confidence.**

As well as the major forms of empowerment listed above, smaller and more personal achievements can give your life shape and enjoyment day by day: going to bed at night knowing you've come one step closer to finishing your novel, achieving your next grade in piano, adding a new section to your carpentry project, or whatever it is that you're most passionate about, is a wonderful feeling. Even completing a difficult crossword can be so satisfying that you'll want to tell everyone about it!

- **Mental stimulation and cognitive health.**

Speaking of crosswords, a study run by Monash University in 2023 of over 10,000 senior Australians found that "certain types of cognitively stimulating leisure activities, including adult literacy and active mental activities, may help prevent dementia in older age" (Wu et al., 2023). The most beneficial activities included writing letters or keeping a journal, taking educational classes, using a computer, playing chess or cards, and doing crosswords or other puzzles (ibid.).

- **Personal fulfilment.**

Identity is a flexible, lifelong project. You may no longer be a CEO, a teacher, a nurse, or whatever you were before you retired, but you can continue to use the skills from your former career (and develop new ones) in a way that brings satisfaction to your life.

- **Social engagement.**

Approximately 28% of Australians over 65 live alone (Senior Lifestyle, 2024b). Loneliness and a sense of isolation are linked with numerous physical and mental health issues (National Academies of Sciences, Engineering, and Medicine, 2020), so it's important to engage with our families, friends and communities regularly. Staying up to date with technology can help you connect with loved ones around the world, and taking your passions and skills out into society by joining social groups (things like book clubs or choirs), and attending local events is a way to make friends and fend off loneliness. You might also find yourself in demand as a teacher for less-experienced members!

Here are some of the avenues available for retirees to pursue their lifelong learning dreams:

7.2 Continuing education at school

Tertiary and other educational institutions offer a wide array of subjects in different formats, including daytime, part-time, weekend and increasingly online. You may want to study informally or to obtain certification or credentials. A quick internet search for courses in your desired subject will bring up a variety of options for you to choose from. Universities, colleges, workshop providers and non-profit organisations are all tapping into the adult education marketplace, offering courses taught by experts in the field.

7.3 Coursera

This is a worldwide online learning platform which offers free, accessible online courses from top universities and leading organisations. You can gain knowledge, skills and certificates through videos, lectures, quizzes and forum discussions. For an additional fee, you can enhance your qualification with a university certificate or degree in a variety of disciplinary subjects. You can find details of course options at www.coursera.org

7.4 The University of the Third Age (U3A)

U3A is a nationwide network of learning groups aimed at encouraging older people to share their knowledge, skills and interests in a friendly environment. There are no assessments and homework, just regular lessons or study groups. The basic idea is learning for fun and not for obtaining qualifications. The group sizes vary according to demand, and they offer a wide choice of academic, creative and leisure activities. It's an ideal way to explore an interest without having to sit exams. You can find details at www.u3amelbcity.org.au

7.5 Virtual fitness classes, apps and eBooks

If you're looking to kickstart healthy habits, there are plenty of courses to choose from. Fitness apps are available for those 50 years and older which provide users with access to gyms nationwide, wellness plans, discounts on massage, acupuncture and other therapies. There are a variety of eBook and audiobook platforms that offer the opportunity to learn more about a topic of interest. (www.storypoint.com)

7.6 Local courses for seniors

www.courses.com.au is a comprehensive website which provides a plethora of short courses for Australian seniors looking to learn new skills and socialise. Its menu offers you a search engine with which to browse courses by subject, qualification and provider close to your home. It also gives you details about government funding. Some of the popular courses on offer are:

- Improve your digital literacy: "Tech Savvy Seniors" is a government-funded program that provides digital training to seniors. Learn how to use computers and smart devices to stay connected with family and friends.
- Vocational training: there are certificate courses on offer in Business Administration, Tourism, Education Support, Early Childhood Education and Care.
- Painting, pottery and ceramics, textiles, fitness and dance, and tonnes more fun classes for seniors.

7.7 Enhancing spirituality in retirement

The University of Divinity (www.divinity.edu.au) excels in education, engagement and research in spiritual practices and Christian beliefs and their contemporary applications. They offer Indigenous studies, Ministry, Philosophy and Theology courses, professional practice education and research, graduate research and provision of infrastructure like library facilities. Students and staff join the University through one of its Colleges or Schools, each of which is a unique learning community. The Colleges are supported by a wide range of churches and religious orders which together resource the University as a whole. Some of the Colleges are:

- Australian Lutheran College
- Catholic Theological College
- Eva Burrows College
- Pilgrim Theological College
- St Athanasius College
- Trinity College Theological School
- Yarra Theological Union

Anne and I have grown tremendously in our Catholic faith in the last few years by subscribing to the following online programs:

- Bible in a Year: Fr Mike Schmitz guides you through the entire Bible in 365 episodes. Using an exclusive reading plan rooted in the Bible Timeline, "you won't just read the Bible, you'll finally understand how all the pieces fit together to tell an amazing story that continues in your life today." This is available on YouTube or as a podcast at www.media.ascensionpress.com
- The Catechism in a Year: Fr Mike Schmitz guides you through the entire Catechism of the Catholic Church in 365 days. "You will understand the essentials of the Catholic faith and why they matter and transform your relationship with the Church that Christ founded." Again, this is available on YouTube or at www.media.ascensionpress.com
- Videos explaining various aspects of the Catholic faith by Fr Chris Alar and Fr Don Calloway are available at their website www.marian.org, or on YouTube
- Word on Fire by Bishop Robert Barron: videos available at www.wordonfire.org or on YouTube.

As ever, the balance of solitary achievement and social engagement that you seek out will depend on your own personality and preferences – you may well find you've earnt a bit of peace and quiet after years spent managing employees and/or children! Yet we are a social species, and we as retirees gain incomparable benefits from sharing our lives with others. Moreover, younger generations gain incomparable benefits from sharing their lives with us. Spiritually, cognitively, emotionally and physically, lifelong learning is a way to safeguard our wellbeing for the rest of our lives.

Chapter 8 – Coping with Ageing

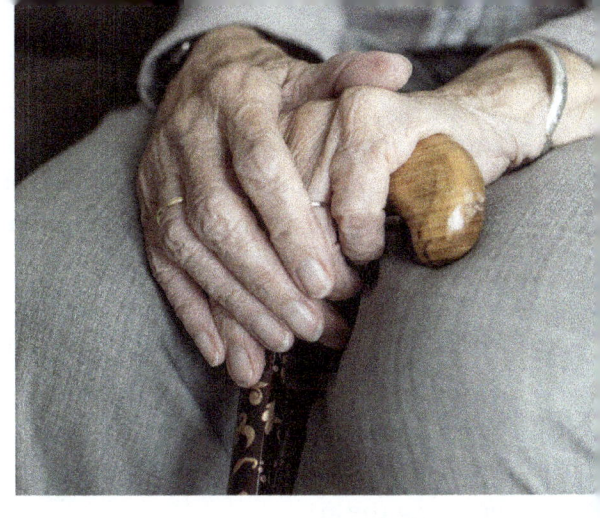

8.1 Introduction

We are all aware that today's society values physical prowess. I have previously discussed in Chapter 2 the importance of remaining physically and mentally fit in retirement, and offered some strategies for doing do. These measures will certainly be beneficial for our health at every age. However, the reality is that even the most physically fit among us will experience a decline in physical capabilities at some stage of our lives. The ageing process tends to reduce our strength, endurance, agility and flexibility, which directly impacts our daily life activities. (Hansen and Haas, 2015, p. 65). It is fair to assume that for majority of us who have retired at 65, the changes in our physical capabilities at 75 might be relatively minor, such as reduced energy levels. A smaller percentage may, however, have witnessed significant physical changes and challenges in that decade of our lives. The key issue is the management of our lives emotionally and spiritually during those trying times of decline in our physical capabilities.

8.2 Living with physical limitations

One of the most challenging things when transitioning to old age is acceptance of the fact that we need help with tasks which we could do by ourselves a few years ago: for example, lifting heavy weights or attending to household chores like cleaning and general maintenance. What happens when the decline in our physical capabilities owing to ageing is not conducive to performing those tasks any longer? Old age imposes limitations on us and we have to learn how to live with them. The "Aging Well" section of HelpGuide.org offers the following advice which can help us cope with the decline in physical capabilities:

- Learn to cope with change: It is important to build resilience and find healthy ways to cope with challenges. This can possibly be achieved by focusing on the things we're grateful for, acknowledging and expressing our feelings, accepting the things we can't change, looking for the silver lining, taking daily action to deal with life's challenges and staying healthy through humour, laughter and play.
- Find meaning and joy: Some of the suggestions are to pick up a long-neglected hobby, learn something new and interesting, get involved in the community, travel somewhere new, and spend time in nature and enjoying the arts.
- Stay connected: Connect regularly with friends and family, make an effort to make new friends, spend time with at least one person every day, volunteer, and find support groups in times of change.
- Stay active and boost vitality. This can be achieved by exercising regularly and by eating and sleeping well.
- Keep the mind sharp: challenge your brain by playing new games or sport, varying your habits and by taking on a completely new subject. (Smith et al., 2024).

8.3 Accepting the reality of our mortality

One of the specific challenges that we face in retirement is coming to grips with our own mortality. Our society generally views death as a distant reality. However, for some of us this realisation may have grown owing

to our involvement with a friend or relative in their final stages of life. For others it may stem from their own illness or injury. Ernest Becker's 1973 book *The Denial of Death* suggests that underlying most if not all of our many attachments, addictions and self-defeating actions and activities is a universal deep denial of our own mortality. He does not claim any specific spiritual dimension to his philosophy, but suggests there must be a connection between our sense of and relationship with the Divine and our ability to live and die peacefully and gracefully. (Quoted in Hansen and Haas, 2015, p.73).

8.4 A spiritual perspective on the decline of physical capabilities in retirement

Some people seem to be at odds with God in wondering "why me?" or "what did I do to deserve this?" Others may accept their problems by feeling that they are a punishment for some wrongdoing in the past. However, there are some who seem to maintain a peace, a sense of humour and a deep compassion and thoughtfulness toward others throughout everything. For them, the loving kindness of God is a real presence. Rather than question or challenge their God, they have a real and profound knowledge of the Divine Presence loving them and even suffering with them. (Hansen and Haas, 2015, p.69).

In the words of Pope Saint John Paul II, in the many different forms it takes, "Suffering seems to be, and is, almost *inseparable from man's earthly existence.*" (*Salvifici Doloris*, section 3, italics in original.) He reminds us, however, that our salvation stems from the suffering of Christ, and therefore "in suffering is contained the greatness of a specific mystery" (ibid., section 4).

"In bringing about the Redemption through suffering, Christ has also raised human suffering to the level of the Redemption. Thus each man, in his suffering, can also become a sharer in the redemptive suffering of Christ." (ibid., section 19).

The question is not an individualistic "why me?" but an experience of life that we share with all other human beings, and with Jesus himself. "When he was abused, he did not return abuse; when he suffered, he did not threaten; but he entrusted himself to the one who judges justly. He himself bore our sins in his body on the cross, so that, free from sins, we might live for righteousness; by his wounds you have been healed." (1 Peter 2:23-24)

While suffering intimidates, writes John Paul II, it also invokes compassion and respect (*Salvifici Doloris*, section 4). There are few things I admire more than someone who has turned their suffering into compassion and set out to help others as a result, and I'm sure many people would agree. Saint Paul tells us to bear each other's burdens (Galatians 6:2), "and in this way you will fulfill the law of Christ." This law is, of course, to love God and our neighbour, just as Jesus did (Mark 12:30-31). When he walked the earth two thousand years ago, Jesus healed sickness and pain wherever he encountered it. They are not part of the world that God declared good when he created it, but a consequence of our own fallen nature, just like ageing and death.

This means that sorrows in life are inevitable, whether physical or mental. What matters is our response to it: whether we become selfish or self-giving. I don't say this lightly: as I mentioned in Chapter 2, I am undergoing treatment for cancer as I write this book. Knowing that Jesus came to earth to experience suffering along with us, and to give it meaning and purpose, is a great comfort to me and my family throughout this process. "For we do not have a high priest who is unable to sympathize with our weaknesses, but we have one who in every respect has been tested as we are, yet without sin." (Hebrews 4:15.)

Therefore, "as the sufferings of Christ abound in us, so our consolation also abounds through Christ." (2 Corinthians 1:5.)

One beautiful form of consolation available to Catholics through the Church is the Anointing of the Sick. Those of my generation may remember 'Extreme Unction' being one of the Seven Sacraments, an anointing with holy oil given to people on their deathbeds. The good news is that these days, you

don't have to be dying to receive it! As the *United States Catholic Catechism for Adults* explains, "The Sacrament of the Anointing of the Sick brings the compassionate presence of Christ into the midst of the sufferings of those who are ill" (2020, p.250). As Jesus healed the sick by touching them, the Church gently places oil on the forehead and hands of those who are ill or in pain. The healing this brings may be physical, but it is more often spiritual: as Jesus said to those he healed, "Go and sin no more," the Anointing of the Sick brings healing from the burdens of sin and sorrow in the soul, and allows the recipient to face their struggles with renewed strength (ibid., p.251). To receive this Sacrament, you can contact your local Catholic parish to ask whether any anointing services are scheduled there, or to ask for a priest to come out to visit you at your home.

It isn't pleasant to think about suffering, or about growing old or becoming sick. As I've shown, there are plenty of measures we can take to extend our years of travel, fun, and independence. Yet, if we live long enough, it's almost inevitable that we will start to experience the effects of old age. This makes it worth taking the time, not only to consider what practical measures we want to put in place in the last years of our lives, but also to think about the person we want to become as we go through that process. We, as elders, should model for younger people what it means to face suffering with kindness, maturity, and dignity. I aim to grow in faith and strength of heart through my present experience with sickness, because, many decades from now, I want my children and grandchildren to remember me as a good man. These memories, too, are part of the legacy we will leave to future generations.

Chapter 9 – A Future Built on Hope

9.1 Introduction

The *Merriam-Webster Dictionary* defines hope as "desire accompanied by expectation of or belief in fulfilment." Hope is an invaluable virtue which we need to possess and harness at all times, especially in our retired lives. While we are bound to face challenges in life, hope provides a boost of motivation and faith that positive change is forthcoming and that every problem has a solution. Overall, hope is beneficial to our wellbeing as it encourages us to persist, even though we may be facing setbacks: "People who visualize a happier future are more likely to make necessary changes when dealing with illness, loss, or life transitions. They can avoid feeling stuck or prolonging their issues by directing their thoughts toward goals." (Johanson, 2024.)

As we transition from pre-retirement times to the final years of our lives, we travel on an emotional journey in which our hope for the future is continuously evolving. I intend to address this changing aspect of our emotional life in 3 distinct phases:

- Phase 1: pre-retirement and early years of retirement (approximately 60 to 70 years);
- Phase 2: the middle years of retired life (approximately 70 to 80 years) and finally
- Phase 3: the golden period of retirement (approximately 80 years and beyond). (Mitchell, 2023)

9.2 Hope-filled future in Phase 1 (approximately 60 to 70 years)

Towards the end of our working lives, we become aware that retirement is on the horizon. Generally, we sort of become disengaged from work as our retirement day nears. When we do retire, the first few years post-retirement are quite challenging. Phase 1 has been often described as the "honeymoon phase" when we have the opportunity to take on new activities on a sort of trial basis (Mitchell, 2023), but figuring out what we actually want to do can be a challenge. The objective is to keep ourselves active and busy and fill the time and space left vacant by our paid employment. The hope for our future during this phase is to manage and strengthen relationships with our spouse or partner. Sometimes we might feel lonely or lose our sense of purpose in life. Prayer and meditation can be beneficial during such times of strife.

As Terry Mitchell (2023) points out, when we meet someone new, one of the first things we ask will often be, "What do you do?" Your changing answers to this question will reflect the process of re-shaping your identity in these years. You might say, "I'm a retired academic/businessman/etc," if you still feel a strong connection to your former work and the way it has shaped your personality. But you might also begin to say things like, "I'm a clean-air campaigner" or "I'm a volunteer at a mental health drop-in centre" or "I'm a writer/artist/musician/tutor" as you branch out into new areas and take on new roles. The question may be social small talk, but your choice of answer isn't necessarily a small thing.

This is why I also see "What do you do?" as a spiritual question. What do you do that gives your life shape and meaning? If you are religious, what do you do to fulfil the purpose for which you believe God placed you on this earth? What gives you hope for the future? (Whether you define "future" as the rest of your own lifespan, or as the future of our planet as a whole.)

Ideally, what we do should come out of who we are. I am a Catholic: what I am is a child of God. That is my main identity from which everything else emerges. Older Catholics may hear the word "vocation" and picture a priest, monk or nun, but a vocation more broadly is what God calls us to do according to our state in life. As such, everyone has a vocation. As a young married man, I was called to raise a family with my wife, and my career was a means to ensure that all of our children's needs could be provided for. Now that our children are grown and I am retired, my vocation is to foster what the Pontifical Council for the Laity calls the "charisms (spiritual gifts) proper to old age," which it defines in *The Dignity of Older People and their Mission in the Church and in the World* (1998) as:

- Disinterestedness. Giving of one's gifts in a way that is not bent toward "efficiency and material success," but with wholehearted generosity and love of one's neighbour.

- Memory. "The younger generations are losing a sense of history and consequently the sense of their own identity" (ibid.) and older people provide a real, living link to the past that can serve as guidance for the future. This document was written in 1998, long before smartphones gave us 24/7 Internet access and further fractured young people's cultural and social identities. Our "digital native" children and grandchildren are drowning in more information than a human being could ever process, with little awareness of how to filter helpful knowledge from damaging lies. People of my generation and older can correct these lies and conspiracy theories, because we were there: we grew up alongside survivors of the Holocaust, for example, and have watched its effects play out across international politics for too many generations to fall for promises of easy solutions to current conflicts. On a lighter note, we also know that Neil Armstrong really did walk on the moon because we were the generation that watched him do it live on television!

- Experience. "Today we live in a world in which the responses of science and technology seem to have supplanted the value of the experience accumulated by older people in the course of their whole lives" (ibid.). We can broaden the scope of our society's knowledge beyond mere utilitarianism, allowing others to find the good, the true and the beautiful in our changing world.
- Interdependence. In the face of "growing individualism and self-seeking," we as older people can "challenge a society in which the weaker are often abandoned" (ibid.). We can stand up for the rights of the poor and sick among our numbers to ensure that no one is left out or their needs neglected.
- A more complete vision of life. The values we bring to our society "include a sense of responsibility, faith in God, friendship, disinterest in power, prudence, patience, wisdom, and a deep inner conviction of the need to respect the creation and foster peace. Older people understand the superiority of 'being' over 'having.'" (ibid.)

In Phase 1 of retirement, we have an opportunity to choose what we want to do with our lives. This in turn helps to shape who we will become in the phases of older age to come.

9.3 Hope-filled future in Phase 2 (approximately 70 to 80 years)

These are the "meat in the sandwich" years of retired life. You might want to evaluate the activities that you have been involved with in the past, and those that have given you the greatest satisfaction and meaning in life. You could selectively continue with some of the past activities and possibly take up some new ones. The most important thing is to get involved in activities that you are passionate about and which bring meaning to your life. Most people find themselves with regular patterns of behaviour. After a year or two you should find yourself comfortably engaged and able to answer questions about your new identity, passion and goals. You start to settle in, as least for the foreseeable future (Mitchell, 2023).

If Phase 1 was about exploration, Phase 2 is about consolidation. By this stage we will have tried many different things. Hopefully we will have found what we're good at, and become experienced in our new post-retirement roles. People often speak of the grief involved in the early phases of retirement, which comes with the loss of our old identity and way of life (Mitchell, 2023; Cagle, 2019). Ideally by Phase 2 we should have reached the resolution of that grief and settled into our new way of life, and with that comes a new energy to devote toward growth and development.

"For we are what he has made us, created in Christ Jesus for good works, which God prepared beforehand to be our way of life." (Ephesians 2:10).

"So then you are no longer strangers and aliens, but you are citizens with the saints and also members of the household of God, built upon the foundation of the apostles and prophets, with Christ Jesus himself as the cornerstone. In him the whole structure is joined together and grows into a holy temple in the Lord; in whom you also are built together spiritually into a dwelling place for God." (Ephesians 2:19-22).

The concept of building on a firm foundation is central to this stage. As Saint Paul says above, our foundation in life is the faith handed down to us by the apostles and prophets. The way we live out our unique vocation in this faith will depend on the way of living we have prepared for ourselves in Phase 1. Phase 1 is our material, emotional and spiritual foundation for Phase 2.

"As Paul VI wrote in *Evangelii Nuntiandi*, modern man 'listens more willingly to witnesses than to teachers, and if he does listen to teachers, it is because they are witnesses.'" (*The Dignity of Older People*, 1998.) We have a lifetime of experience and knowledge, and once we have found our feet in post-retirement life, we are ready to deepen our witness to the world around us.

9.4 Hope-filled future in Phase 3 (approximately 80 years and beyond)

This is the golden period of retirement: a time for you to reflect and savour your past, live in the present and look with hope into the future. During this time there is generally quite a noticeable decline in our physical and mental capabilities, which means that relationships are more important than ever. Work out a plan in which you and your spouse or partner can continue to grow and pursue your life together and separately as appropriate. You will find you are more interested in your family: children, grandchildren, siblings, cousins. Go for visits and invite them to visit you. Reach out to neighbours, people at church and new people you meet along the way (Mitchell, 2023).

With respect to spirituality, I would like to quote excerpts from an interview with Sister Joan, a Franciscan sister (Hansen and Haas, 2015, p.86) who has this to say:

> Since I have come to live in a retirement home, planning for the future has taken on a much more focused faith-life component. The reflective moment has become a way of life for me. Daily I am aware that time is my future as it always has been. The same questions come to me: Who am I? Who am I becoming? My faith life tells me that I am a valuable person, a child of God who is loved unconditionally by a merciful God. I spend time recalling the good times of the past as I move into the future. It is heartwarming to reminisce and tell my story of the past and remember the good.

She goes on to write about embracing life, and "the gifts of person that have not changed." I see this as an excellent framework for a discussion of hope during the ageing process. Often when you speak with people in their eighties and nineties, they will tell you that they don't feel that age inside: they still feel more or less like the people they were at twenty or thirty. They have more life experience now than they did back then, and although the mirror certainly reflects the passing of the years, the person inside remains the same as they've always been.

As the famous question goes, "How old would you be if you didn't know how old you are?"

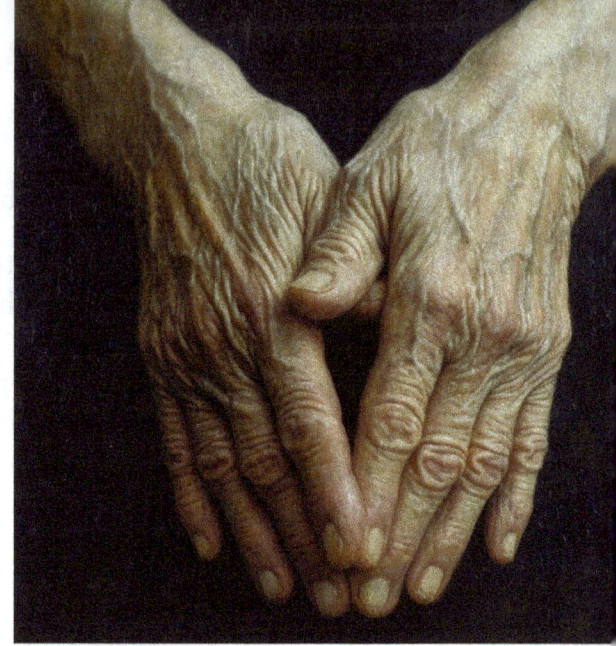

At the moment, undergoing treatment for cancer, I am certainly feeling my age! But up until my diagnosis and the beginning of my treatment, I felt perhaps 40 or 50. The important thing is that I reminisce on all the good times of my life right from my early school days and feel blessed to have had a great life overall. As the Pontifical Council for the Laity expressed it, "Only in the light of the faith, strengthened by the hope which does not deceive (cf. *Rom* 5:5), shall we be able to accept old age in a truly Christian way both as a gift and a task. That is the secret of the youthfulness of spirit, which we can continue to cultivate in spite of the passing of years." (*The Dignity of Older People*, 1998.) My faith gives me strength and hope for the future, as well as the ability to see the hand of God as it has shaped my life so far.

This ability to look forward as well as back is an essential component of hope, because it reminds us that there is always so much more in life to learn and embrace, just as there was when we were in our twenties. The body may not be as forgiving of being knocked around as it was when we were younger, so it pays to be a bit more cautious in our approach to various activities. But that doesn't mean we can't continue to try things that will help us to grow in knowledge and experience. This can be a physical process of learning new activities and skills, or it can be a mental or spiritual experience, exploring the nature of your own mind, heart and soul more thoroughly than ever before.

Sister Joan writes, "If I am to love my neighbour as myself, then I must love all that is me, and be willing to share myself with them. The spiritual challenge I am facing now is learning to embrace my life here and be willing to share the depths of my soul." (Hansen and Haas, 2015, p.88)

I wrote in Chapter 2 about the examination of conscience that I make each day. This isn't always easy, but being honest with myself and with God about my spiritual progress is important. What Sister Joan describes here is similar. It's not a pointless dredging-up of old memories, but a conscious process of facing and coming to peace with the experiences of a lifetime. Perhaps there were things I could have done better in the past, if I'd had the knowledge and resources back then that I have now. It takes courage to look at those things honestly. But letting go of guilt from the past is an important part of hope for the future, because it's an acknowledgement that I'm not limited by my past mistakes. I can keep growing and changing.

"What do you do?"

This is a question about vocation as well as the way we occupy our time from day to day. As we progress through each of the three phases I described above, our answer will develop and mature. My essential identity is always who I am in the eyes of God, and what I do to help my neighbour is a reflection of that. We must "look to God throughout our whole life, since he is the goal to which our human pilgrimage is always directed," (*The Dignity of Older People*, 1998), and no stage of life is too late to choose what sort of person we want to be in response to his love.

Chapter 10 – Wills and Related Affairs

10.1 Introduction

In the foregoing chapters, we have discussed pertinent issues associated with happier retired lives. This is all fine; however, we are mortal beings and will one day have to face the ultimate reality. Having worked so hard throughout our lives, it is only natural to plan how to distribute our wealth after we have gone, and also to have some contingencies in place for our end-of-life scenarios. This chapter will address those somewhat thorny issues in a logical and meaningful sequence.

10.2 Last Will and Testament

A will is a legal document that sets out what you want to happen to your assets after you die. These assets are called your estate, and may include your house, land, car, money, personal effects, investments, and superannuation. A will needs to be prepared and written in the right way be legally valid. It should be reviewed and updated as circumstances change. It is best to ask a lawyer to advise you, or to contact the Public Trustee in your state. If you die without a will, you are said to die intestate, and your assets will then be distributed to family members according to a formula provided by law. Any will can be challenged in court, but having a valid will usually means your assets will go to whomever you want, which avoid costs and simplifies things for your family (Cancer Council NSW, 2021).

10.3 Enduring Power of Attorney

This document allows you to appoint someone to make financial and personal decisions on your behalf if you no longer have the capacity to make them yourself. You can only prepare this document while you still have the capacity to make your own decisions. You can specify when this document comes into effect and the enduring power of attorney begins: immediately, on a certain date, or not until you lose decision-making capacity. In this third case, it will begin when your appointed attorney believes that you no longer have the capacity to manage your own financial decisions, or when your doctor assesses you as no longer having the capacity to make decisions. (Compass, 2024.)

10.4 Advance Care Directive

This involves formally detailing your values and preferences regarding your future healthcare. This document is legally binding if you signed it when you had legal capacity. It may include things like:

- Whether you wish to be resuscitated or not
- Whether you consent to being placed on a life support machine, and if so, for how long

- Whether you consent to other life-prolonging treatments (for example, tube-feeding) and if so, in what circumstances you would wish these measures to be removed
- Whether you wish to be an organ donor. (Advance Care Planning, January 2024)

Your doctor and loved ones cannot override directions stated in this document. According to the advice provided by HealthDirect, "You don't need a lawyer for this to be valid, but you will need witnesses to sign it when you do. It is also a good idea for your substitute decision-maker and doctor to sign the form. A substitute decision-maker is a person who will be legally able to make decisions on your behalf about your healthcare if you can't." (Health Direct, April 2023.)

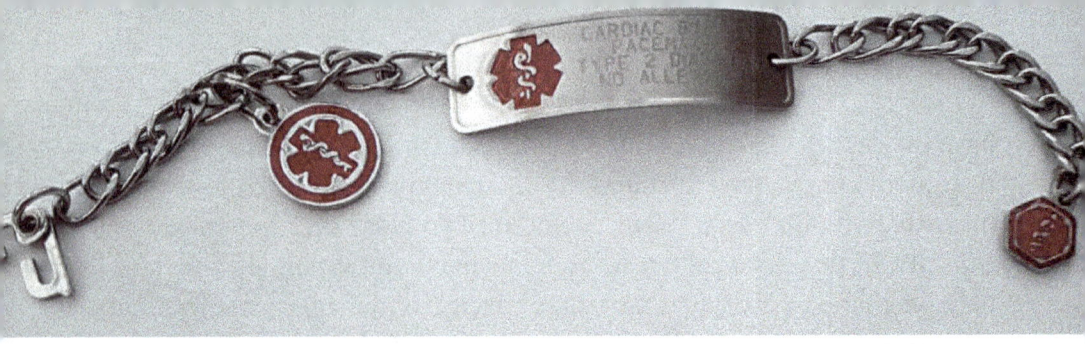

If you have medical issues that first responders will need to know about in an emergency – a heart condition, for example, or osteoporosis, or an allergy to certain medications – then you may wish to apply for a MedicAlert account. You can register the details of your medical conditions and needs with MedicAlert, and then order a bracelet or necklace with the most important information engraved and a code that those treating you can use to access your complete record. You will also receive a card printed with this information that you can place in your wallet or purse. Many hospitals and pharmacies will have paper forms that you can fill out to apply for MedicAlert, or you can register online or over the phone. They are "the only emergency medical information service endorsed by paramedics across Australia" (MedicAlert, 2024), and have been providing this service for over fifty years. It is not expensive to register, and saves lives.

It is important to ensure that your next of kin and nominated representatives know where to find your Enduring Power of Attorney and Advanced Care Directive documents, as well as your current legal will. If you have a prepaid funeral plan, or choose to make a statement concerning your preferences over where and how you would like to be buried or cremated, these documents should be easily available to them as well. A Catholic may wish to ensure that their children know that they want to have a funeral Mass rather than a secular ceremony, for example, and that the Church does not permit the scattering of cremated remains.

You may also choose to leave a document detailing your digital passwords (for example, your phone and computer access codes, as well as email, online banking and social media login details) in a secure location so that your next of kin or nominated representatives will not be locked out of your accounts after your death.

10.5 Spirituality associated with end-of-life scenarios

As we approach the end of our lives, our views on spirituality may change as we begin to think about our lives in a new way and reflect on the meaning of life. Our spiritual needs at this critical juncture of our lives can include:

- Connecting with the faith and practices of our religion
- Understanding what gives our life meaning
- Exploring how we wish to be remembered
- Asking for forgiveness for ourselves
- Offering forgiveness to others
- Sharing our life story (Crossroads, 2024).

As for me, I truly believe that there is life everlasting after my death. This is justified by the fact that Jesus rose from the dead and that he will come again to judge the living and the dead at the end of time.

It is natural to feel some nervousness about death, "the undiscovered country from whose bourn no traveller returns," as Shakespeare called it. However, the faith that I practise as a Catholic is one based in trust and love: after I die, I will be reunited with the God who made me, and who loves me.

In the words of the Nicene Creed, which we repeat every Sunday at Mass: "I look forward to the resurrection of the dead and the life of the world to come." Not just that we accept the inevitability of death, but that we look forward with joy to the eternal life that will follow it. Jesus told us that there are many rooms in his Father's house (John 14:2), and that he has gone before us to prepare a place for us there. This is the Good News of our salvation: "We have been buried with him by baptism into death, so that, just as Christ was raised from the dead by the glory of the Father, so we too might walk in newness of life. For if we have been united with him in a death like his, we will certainly be united with him in a resurrection like his." (Romans 6:4-5.)

Through prayer and the sacraments, we can live in a state of friendship with God while we are alive. In this way, we will be ready whenever he calls us home to him, and can go to him as our loving Father.

Chapter 11 – Closing Comments

11.1 Motivation for writing this book

I have reviewed a number of books and articles which purport to address issues relating to preparation for a happy retirement, which invariably discuss inter-alia, finances, health and wellbeing, travel, relationships and activities. You will have seen many of them quoted throughout the book because of the sound practical guidance that they contain. However, as I noted in the Introduction, discussion of the spiritual dimension in retirement is conspicuously absent from these publications. I believe this is a significant oversight. Religion, and spirituality in general, provides a positive framework for considering the challenges and opportunities present at every stage of ageing, and for exploring the deeper meanings of events in our lives. This is why I have drawn material from Scripture, religious authors, and Church documents into my work alongside the existing literature on preparing for retirement: to show how a sense of the sacred can complement the practical actions we take to maintain our health and independence into old age. Anne and I have been fortunate and blessed to have harnessed in a small way that gift, which for us has been the cornerstone of our retired lives.

11.2 Post surgery, recovery and moving forward

As explained earlier in Chapter 2, in recent months Anne and I have been faced with what has possibly been the greatest trial of our lives. About two weeks prior to my surgery, I had to undergo several scans, blood tests, MRIs and nuclear medicine imaging. Our spiritual fortitude and prayer life are helping us to wade through this difficult period with considerable ease. No financial or other resources could have ever given us this solace and peace of mind that everything would be fine. On the day of the surgery, we abandoned ourselves completely to God. In our hearts and minds, Jesus was there to guide the surgeon throughout every step of the twelve-hour process. The surgery went extremely well, and I was discharged from the hospital in five days, which according to the surgeon was half the average discharge time for people my age. Now I am in the recovery phase, with further treatment to follow shortly. By the grace of God, we hope to be doing what we love to do in the near future, i.e. travel overseas. If it is his will, Anne and I would like to undertake our second Camino walk.

In the introductory chapter, I provided a brief synopsis of the story of my life. As you've seen, I have had an interesting working life, changing careers and travelling around the globe. This has given me a varied perspective on life, and I have drawn on my own experiences to show the important role that my faith has played in facing the challenges of work and retirement. As someone who has spent a lifetime filling the different roles that God has given me — son, husband, father, grandfather — when I speak of vocation, it is with the aim of urging other retirees to look at the vital part they have played in the life of their own communities, and the exciting new roles that they can embrace for the future.

As Pope John Paul II said to a crowd of over 8000 older people in 1984, "You are not and must not consider yourselves to be on the margins of the life of the Church, passive elements in a world in excessive motion, but active subjects of a period in human existence which is rich in spirituality and humanity. You still have a mission to fulfil and a contribution to make." (*The Dignity of Older People*, 1998.)

I have enjoyed sharing my own experiences of the goodness and mercy of God throughout my life with you, and I hope that you will be inspired to share your own story with others in turn.

> *So even to old age and gray hairs,*
> *O God, do not forsake me,*
> *until I proclaim your might*
> *to all the generations to come.*
>
> **Psalm 71:18**

11.3 The changing landscape throughout retired life

The circumstances and aspirations of the retired community are dynamic, and evolve throughout their retired lives. The three phases of retired life that I have suggested — Phase 1 for persons between 60 and 70 years, Phase 2 for persons between 70 and 80 years and Phase 3 for persons between 80 and beyond — are by no means exhaustive. However, they aim to delineate the changing landscape of our physical, mental and spiritual well-being in a simple way, and offer a framework for exploring the ways in which our priorities in life change at different stages of life. What we want to do and be at sixty will likely be quite different from what we want at seventy, eighty, ninety or a hundred. No matter what our age, however, we will always want to live a life that is dignified, meaningful, and shared with people we love. My purpose in writing this book was to suggest ways to approach each stage of life to make this a joyful reality.

I sincerely hope that this book gives you, by the grace of God, some ideas and thoughts that will make your retirement a very enjoyable and spirit-filled one. As we age, we can grow closer to Christ and to others. Far from being burdensome, this life with God can be our greatest adventure of all.

God bless you always!

Gray hair is a crown of glory;
it is gained in a righteous life.

Proverbs 16:31

Bibliography

Introduction:

Spirituality. (n.d.). In *Oxford English Dictionary.* Retrieved from https://www.oed.com/search/dictionary/?scope=Entries&q=spirituality

Waaijiman, K. (2002). *Spirituality: Forms, foundations, methods.* (J. Vriend, Trans.). Peeters Publishers Leuven.

Saucier, G. & Skrzypinska, K. (2006). Spiritual but not religious? Evidence for two independent dispositions. *Journal of Personality*, 74(5), 1257-1292. https://doi.org/10.1111/j.1467-6494.2006.00409.x

Sheldrake, P. (2007). *A brief history of spirituality.* Wiley.

Wong, Y. & Vinsky, J. (2009). Speaking from the margins: A critical reflection on the 'spiritual-but-not-religious' discourse in social work. *British Journal of Social Work*, 39(7), 1343-1359. https://doi.org/10.1093/bjsw/bcn032

Faith. (n.d.). In *Oxford English Dictionary.* Retrieved from https://www.oed.com/search/dictionary/?scope=Entries&q=faith

Religion. (n.d.). In *Oxford English Dictionary.* Retrieved from https://www.oed.com/search/dictionary/?scope=Entries&q=religion

Caldwell, S. (2024, April 5). 'I'm a cultural Christian', declares Richard Dawkins, the world's most famous atheist. *Catholic Herald.* https://catholicherald.co.uk/im-a-cultural-christian-declares-richard-dawkins-the-worlds-most-famous-atheist/

Chapter 1: Finances

Shaw, R. (2016, July 31). Understanding Detachment. *The Catholic Thing.* https://www.thecatholicthing.org/2016/07/31/understanding-detachment/

New Revised Standard Version, Catholic Edition. (1993). https://www.biblegateway.com/versions/New-Revised-Standard-Version-Catholic-Edition-NRSVCE-Bible/#booklist

Cresp, Sr. M. (2020, November 8). St Mary MacKillop – The Pilgrim. https://www.sosj.org.au/footsteps-mary-mackillop-20/

Ferguson, S. (2023, January 6). What is Discernment? *Ligioner.* https://www.ligonier.org/learn/articles/discernment-thinking-gods-thoughts

Chapter 2: Health and Wellbeing:

Cherry, K. (2023, February 28). Integrity vs. despair in psychosocial development. *VeryWell Mind*. https://www.verywellmind.com/integrity-versus-despair-2795738

HealthDirect. (2024). *Mediterranean Diet*. https://www.healthdirect.gov.au/mediterranean-diet#:~:text=There%20are%20many%20health%20benefits,processed%20foods%20and%20red%20meat.

World Health Organization. (2022). *Mental health*. https://www.who.int/news-room/fact-sheets/detail/mental-health-strengthening-our-response

Suni, E., & Dimitriu, J. (2024, March 26). Mental health and sleep. *Sleep Foundation*. https://www.sleepfoundation.org/mental-health

Walden University. (2024). *The power of smiling*. https://www.waldenu.edu/online-bachelors-programs/bs-in-psychology/resource/the-power-of-smiling#:~:text=You%20feel%20better%20when%20you%20smile.&text=And%20because%20you%20typically%20smile,that%20relieves%20pain%20and%20stress.

Mindful Staff. (2020, July 8). What is Mindfulness? *Mindful*. https://www.mindful.org/what-is-mindfulness/

Rasmussen, Sr. John Dominic. (2023, February 21). The three forms of prayer. *Openlight Media*. https://openlightmedia.com/2023/the-three-forms-of-prayer/

St. Hilaire, L. (2019, September 11). *An introduction to the types of prayer*. St Paul Centre for Biblical Theology. https://stpaulcenter.com/an-introduction-to-the-types-of-prayer/

Szyszkiewicz, B. (2023, December 23). Prayer as intercession. *Simply Catholic*. https://www.simplycatholic.com/prayer-as-intercession/

Adversity. (n.d.). In *Collins Dictionary Online*. Retrieved from https://www.collinsdictionary.com/dictionary/english/adversity

Chapter 3: Travel

Youth Voices. (2020, October 30). *The importance of pilgrimages*. https://www.youthvoices.live/the-importance-of-pilgrimages/

Bergeron, M. (2024, April 12). Marilyn Bergeron: Eucharistic miracles show the continuing reality of its power. *Standard-Freeholder*. https://www.standard-freeholder.com/opinion/columnists/marilyn-bergeron-eucharistic-miracles-show-the-continuing-reality-of-its-power

Thoman, B. (2022, May 24). Loreto and the Holy House of Mary. *National Catholic Register*. https://www.ncregister.com/blog/the-holy-house-of-loreto-italy

Dufaur, L. (2016, August 7). *Science confirms: Angels took the House of Our Lady of Nazareth to Loreto*. The American Society for the Defense of Tradition, Family, and Property. https://www.tfp.org/science-confirms-angels-took-the-house-of-our-lady-of-nazareth-to-loreto/

Chapter 4: Activities

Ackerman, C. (2018, April 20). *What is Positive Psychology & why is it important?* https://positivepsychology.com/what-is-positive-psychology-definition/

National Center for Complementary and Integrative Health. (2022, September.) *Music and health: What you need to know.* https://www.nccih.nih.gov/health/music-and-health-what-you-need-to-know

Australian Men's Shed Association. (2024). Welcome to AMSA. https://mensshed.org/

Beck, R. (2020, July 14). The law of the gift. *Experimental Theology*. https://experimentaltheology.blogspot.com/2020/07/the-law-of-gift.html

Barron, Bishop R. (2017, November 19.) Parable of the talents. *Word on Fire*. https://www.wordonfire.org/videos/sermons/parable-of-the-talents/

United States Catholic Conference of Bishops. (2020). *United States Catholic Catechism for adults* (2nd ed.). Retrieved from https://www.usccb.org/sites/default/files/flipbooks/uscca/files/assets/basic-html/page-1.html#

Chapter 5: Building and Maintaining Relationships

Accord. (2024). Impact of retirement on marriages and relationships. https://www.accord.ie/resources/articles/impact-of-retirement-on-marriages-and-relationships

Hansen, J. & Haass, J. (2016). *Retirement as a spiritual pilgrimage: Stories, Scripture and practices for the journey*. CreateSpace Independent Publishing Platform.

Geiger, A.W. (2016, November 30). *Sharing chores a key to good marriage, say majority of married adults*. https://www.pewresearch.org/short-reads/2016/11/30/sharing-chores-a-key-to-good-marriage-say-majority-of-married-adults/

Qualls, M. (2021, September 22). *Do my spouse and I need common interests?* https://firstthings.org/common-interests-spouse/

Firestone, L. (2016). *Just be kind: The only relationship advice you'll ever need.* https://www.psychalive.org/just-be-kind-the-only-relationship-advice-youll-ever-need/

Marriage Encounter Australia. (2024). *About World Wide Marriage Encounter.* https://www.wwme.org.au/about

US Conference of Catholic Bishops. (2018, May). *To love is to will the good of others.* https://www.usccb.org/issues-and-action/marriage-and-family/natural-family-planning/resources/upload/HV-2018-May-Will-The-Good.pdf

Osteen, S., & Neel, R. (2018). *Couples and money: Let's talk about it.* https://extension.okstate.edu/fact-sheets/couples-and-money-lets-talk-about-it.html

Cruze, R. (2024, February 9). *Money & marriage: 7 tips for a healthy relationship.* https://www.ramseysolutions.com/relationships/the-truth-about-money-and-relationships#:~:text=It's%20crucial%20to%20be%20open,why%20you're%20doing%20it.

Watson, E. (2023, November 8). *KIPPERS: Have you got some at home?* https://www.elliotwatson.com.au/kippers-have-you-got-some/

Gill, J. (2024, January 8). *Family dynamics in retirement: How can I nurture relationships without overstepping?* https://www.linkedin.com/pulse/family-dynamics-retirement-how-can-i-nurture-without-jeff-gill-maiaf?trk=article-ssr-frontend-pulse_more-articles_related-content-card

Ware, B. (2012). *The top five regrets of the dying: A life transformed by the dearly departing.* Hay House.

Chapter 6: The Gift of Nature

Weir, K. (2020, April 1). Nurtured by nature. *Monitor on Psychology,* 51(3). https://www.apa.org/monitor/2020/04/nurtured-nature#:~:text=And%20experiments%20have%20found%20that,5%2C%202019).

Rogers, K. (2023, June 13). Biophilia hypothesis. *Encyclopedia Britannica.* https://www.britannica.com/science/biophilia-hypothesis

Heybridge, T. (2021). *The retirement handbook.* Summersdale.

Jimenez, M. P., DeVille, N. V., Elliott, E. G., Schiff, J. E., Wilt, G. E., Hart, J. E., & James, P. (2021). Associations between nature exposure and health: A review of the evidence. *International journal of environmental research and public health,* 18(9), 4790. https://doi.org/10.3390/ijerph18094790

Japan National Tourist Organization. (2024) *Forest bathing in Japan.* https://www.japan.travel/en/guide/forest-bathing/

The International Ecotourism Society. (2006). *TIES global Ecotourism fact sheet.* https://www.researchgate.net/profile/Chaminda-Kumara-5/post/Where-can-I-find-accurate-statistics-about-the-best-ecotourism-destinations-in-which-some-details-about-the-number-of-arrivals-are-mentioned/attachment/59d645e979197b80779a0f94/AS%3A455170728435714%401485532566915/download/1.PDF

Canadian Space Agency. (2021, June 17). *Stargazing tips.* https://www.asc-csa.gc.ca/eng/astronomy/tips-tricks/stargazing-tips.asp

Stiteler, S. *Birdchick.* https://www.birdchick.com/

Caritas Australia (2022). *Care for our common home.* https://www.caritas.org.au/learn/cst-toolkit/care-for-our-common-home/

Chapter 7: Lifelong Learning

Senior Lifestyle. (2024a). *Why lifelong learning is important for seniors.* https://www.seniorlifestyle.com/resources/blog/lifelong-learning-for-seniors/#:~:text=Cognitive%20decline%20is%20a%20natural,excellent%20means%20of%20mental%20stimulation.

Kollmorgen, A. (2023, July 25). *Older Australians most affected by scams.* Choice Australia. https://www.choice.com.au/health-and-body/healthy-ageing/ageing-and-retirement/articles/scams-affecting-senior-australians#:~:text=Losses%20increased%20from%202021%20to%202022&text=People%20aged%2065%20and%20over,%2C%20up%2047%25%20from%202021

Wu, Z., Pandigama, D., Wrigglesworth, J., Owen, A., Woods, R., Chong, T., Orchard, S., Shah, R., Sheets, K., McNeil, J., Murray, A., Ryan, J. (2023, June 14). Lifestyle enrichment in later life and its association with dementia risk. *JAMA Network Open*, 6(7), 2323690. doi:10.1001/jamanetworkopen.2023.23690

Senior Lifestyle. (2024b). *What is senior isolation, and what can you do to help?* https://www.seniorlifestyle.com/resources/blog/what-is-senior-isolation/

National Academies of Sciences, Engineering, and Medicine. (2020). *Social isolation and loneliness in older adults: Opportunities for the health care system.* Washington, DC: The National Academies Press. https://doi.org/10.17226/25663

Victorian Government. (2022, 28 June). *Priority action area 2: Tech-Savvy Seniors.*

https://www.vic.gov.au/ageing-well-action-plan/what-government-will-do-ageing-well-victoria-action-plan/priority-action-2-tech-savvy-seniors

Chapter 8: Coping with Ageing

Smith, M., Segal, J., White, M., (2024, February 5). *Aging well.* https://www.helpguide.org/articles/alzheimers-dementia-aging/staying-healthy-as-you-age.htm#:~:text=As%20well%20as%20learning%20to,also%20brings%20anxiety%20and%20fear.

John Paul II. (1984, February 11). *Salvifici Doloris.* https://www.vatican.va/content/john-paul-ii/en/apost_letters/1984/documents/hf_jp-ii_apl_11021984_salvifici-doloris.html

Chapter 9: A Future Built on Hope

Hope. (2024, April 20). In *Merriam-Webster Dictionary.* Retrieved from https://www.merriam-webster.com/dictionary/hope?utm_campaign=sd&utm_medium=serp&utm_source=jsonld

Johanson, A. (2024, February 8). *Why is hope important?* https://www.choosingtherapy.com/why-is-hope-important/

Mitchell, T. (2023, September). *The retirement process: A psychological and emotional journey.* https://retirees.uw.edu/resources/retirement-transitions/the-retirement-process-a-psychological-and-emotional-journey/

Pontifical Council for the Laity. (1998, October 1). *The dignity of older people and their mission in the Church and in the world.* https://www.vatican.va/roman_curia/pontifical_councils/laity/documents/rc_pc_laity_doc_05021999_older-people_en.html

Cagle, C. (2019, April 10). *The retirement "identity crisis" – a biblical perspective.* https://retirementstewardship.com/2019/04/10/the-retirement-identity-crisis-a-biblical-perspective/

Quote Investigator (2021, August 24). *How old would you be if you didn't know how old you are?* https://quoteinvestigator.com/2021/08/24/how-old/

Chapter 10: Wills and Related Affairs

Cancer Council NSW. (2021). *Preparing legal documents.*
https://www.cancercouncil.com.au/cancer-information/advanced-cancer/end-of-life/practical-concerns/preparing-legal-documents/

Compass (2024, April 26). *Enduring power of attorney in Victoria.*
https://www.compass.info/featured-topics/powers-of-attorney/victoria/

Advance Care Planning Australia (2024, January). *Create your plan in Victoria.*
https://www.advancecareplanning.org.au/create-your-plan/create-your-plan-vic

HealthDirect (2023, April). *Advance care planning and directive.*
https://www.healthdirect.gov.au/advance-care-planning-and-directive#substitute

MedicAlert (2024). *How the MedicAlert Foundation makes a difference.*
https://www.medicalert.org.au/about-us

Crossroads Hospice and Palliative Care (2024). *Spirituality & end-of-life care.*
https://www.crossroadshospice.com/hospice-resources/spirituality-end-of-life-care/

www.ingramcontent.com/pod-product-compliance
Lightning Source LLC
Chambersburg PA
CBHW072022060426
42449CB00034B/1825